JOE GIRARD
WITH ROBERT CASEMORE

MASTERING YOUR WAY TO THE TOP

SECRETS FOR SUCCESS FROM THE WORLD'S GREATEST SALESMAN AND AMERICA'S LEADING BUSINESSPEOPLE

WARNER BOOKS

A Time Warner Company

Warner Books, Inc., 1271 Avenue of the Americas, New York, NY 10020
New York, NY 10020

W A Time Warner Company

Printed in the United States of America
First Printing: February 1995
10 9 8 7 6 5 4 3 2 1

Library of Congress Cataloging-in-Publication Data

Girard, Joe.
    Mastering your way to the top : secrets for success from the
world's greatest salesman and America's leading business people /
Joe Girard with Robert Casemore.
        p.   cm.
    Includes bibliographical references.
    ISBN 0-446-51674-0
    1. Selling. 2. Success in business—United States. 3. Sales
executives—United States. 4. Businessmen—United States. 5. Women
in business—United States. I. Casemore, Robert. II. Title.
HF5438.25.G573   1995
658.85—dc20   94-13593
                                                                     CIP

Book design by H. Roberts

Dedicated to my family:
Kitty, my wife
Joe and Patty, my son and daughter-in-law
Grace, my daughter
June, Joey, and Matthew, my grandchildren
Tina Ringer, my sister
Marie Addis, my mother-in-law
and Jennie Kranik, my very dearest friend
I love you all very much!

Contents

MASTERING YOUR WAY TO THE TOP

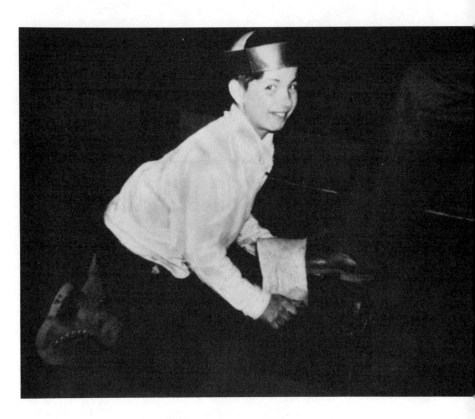

Joe Girard, February 1939
"You never want to forget where you came from!"

1
How You
See Yourself

MOST MEN WHO shave with a blade razor each morning see themselves in the bathroom mirror. If they look at their faces critically, it's probably to make sure they don't cut themselves. They also sneak a glance or two at their figures as they pass by a store's plate-glass window. Maybe they suck in their guts, hoping that a thirty-eight-inch waist really looks like a thirty-four. Right? You bet.

Nearly all women give their bathroom mirrors full attention when they put on their morning makeup. Several times during the day and evening they haul out compacts and lipstick to give their cheeks, eyelids, and lips a touchup.

One way or another, we all get glimpses of ourselves daily. Mostly it's by our own choosing, or perhaps accidentally, or maybe "accidentally on purpose." In life there's always something or someone on hand to give us a playback of ourselves. A reflection in a pool of water, the rear- and side-view mirrors on a set of wheels, another person's reaction to something we've said or done.

It's not what you see yourself *in* but, rather, what you see yourself *as* that counts—your image. Ask yourself: How do I see myself? A failure? Poor me? Just getting by? Hanging in there? Flat-out successful?

If you see *success*, great. You've earned it. As the song by Cole Porter goes, "You're the Top." On a scale of 1 to 10, that's a 10! If you see yourself in the mirror as anything less than that, even a 9, you need help in getting to the top.

You need me. Whether you're a man or a woman, whether you're young or not so young, you need me. Joe Girard.

You Are Number One

Don't confuse that 10 rating on the scale with being number one. For years I've told my readers and those who've attended my lectures: "*You* are number one, *numero uno*, the most important person in the world." I wear a "No. 1" gold lapel pin. I've given away thousands of such pins to people who stand up at my conventions, or who came up from the audience to stand by me on a lecture platform, and who shout proudly, "*I am number one!*"

I learned at a very early age that achieving success, that reaching the top, depended on *my* efforts alone. I realized that it was up to me to look out for number one. Nobody else was going to bother. Other successful businesspeople tell me that the same holds true for them.

Once that conviction is firmly established in *your* mind, you're ready to take the steps that help you reach the top. You not only take them, but *master* them. And you have a great time, a rewarding time, doing so.

You can reach the top in your chosen profession, whatever it may be. Or you can achieve success in a different line of work; nothing says you can't steer your career boat in another direction if you want to. The choice is yours: be at the top in your present job or in a new job; reach your present goals or head for new goals.

For example, I began my career as a salesperson with nothing to start me on my way but a telephone, a phone book, and a dusty desk in an upstairs vacant corner of a car dealership. From that humble beginning I took many steps toward success and *mastered* them.

From 1966 to 1977, I was the number one retail car salesperson in the world. Luck? No, it was smart work. By the time I retired from selling I had sold 13,001 new cars, all at retail—sometimes over 170 a month. In 1973 alone, I sold 1,425 cars, again at retail and not fleet sales, and all belly-to-belly—a feat that put me in the *Guinness Book of Records*. As of this date, the record—that "top"—has not been broken. But when that happens, I'll be the first to step up and shake the hand of the salesperson who does it.

If I Can Do It, So Can You

It's said that Alexander the Great, the Macedonian general who conquered Persia, cried because he saw no new worlds to conquer. Hogwash! There are always more worlds—new worlds—to battle and subdue.

I made a career change. I started writing, and my three books have been and continue to be best-sellers, with over 3 million copies sold. In *How to Sell Anything to Anybody*, *How to Close Every Sale*, and *How to Sell Yourself*, I simply passed along some of the many selling strategies that helped me get into the *Guinness Book of Records*. Happily, at the same time I reached another top, so I began a new career as an international lecturer.

Are there any worlds left for me to conquer? You bet. For the past several years I have appeared before large and enthusiastic audiences throughout the United States and in Canada, Australia and New Zealand, many European countries, Central America, Malaysia, and Indonesia. Once again I'm heading for a new top, with the chance to teach others the steps I've mastered and the things I've learned along the way. These steps helped me in my business; they'll help you in yours.

My challenge to readers and audiences has always been: If I can do it, so can you! But I've added something that not very many folks want to hear. To people who want to zoom to the top without taking the important steps to get there, I've reminded my audiences, "You've got to climb to the top one step at a time, because the elevator is out of order." The sign in my office advises me to always take the stairs.

The Importance of Looking Back

One of the finest stories about climbing to the top was related to me by a sales manager of a car dealership in Scandinavia. A few years ago I gave a talk to a group of directors and managers at an international sales conference. This particular fellow sat in the front row, and seemed to hang on to every word I said. Sometimes he smiled, sometimes he frowned.

I told a story of two mountain climbers who, upon reaching a summit in the Alps, one a little ahead of the other, paused to compare notes. The slower one said that he always felt important when he got to the top. "I look below at the villages in the valley. I see how insignificant other human beings seem to be. They move along like ants, but I'm king of the ant hill." The other climber said, "I beat you here because I know of a shortcut, a mountain pass. The climbers behind me didn't. I feel proud of myself that I got to the top faster and easier than you. That's what's really important."

What's the point? There are differences in the time it takes to get to the top and differences in the satisfaction one feels upon getting there. That was all. I had not touched upon what to do or not do, what to think about or not think about, on the way to the top.

The fellow in the front row noticed that, and at the close of the conference he approached me. I guessed him to be in his mid-forties. He introduced himself and said that his hobby—his sport—was mountain climbing. This was easy to believe. He looked tan and physically fit—a blond Viking. He said, "Mr. Girard . . ."

"Call me Joe."

"All right, Joe. I just wanted to say that when I get to the top of any mountain peak *I've* climbed, I don't look down on the small, earthbound creatures below. I don't keep watch of the climber behind me unless we're working as a roped-together team, where my life might well depend upon my teammate. I look back only to see *where I was* at every ledge and at every crevice—at every spot where I paused to get a firm hand grip or to make sure of a solid foothold. I want to remember what the mountain can teach me. I look back only at *myself* because I'm the only one who's responsible for me. And that's the way I do my job. I look back at the many steps I've taken and mastered, and I look ahead to the steps to come."

Then he lightened up a bit and grinned. "The elevator isn't out of order, Joe. For mountain climbers, it's the funicular that isn't working."

I hate big words, especially if I don't know what they mean. I asked him, "What the devil's a funicular?" Where I grew up in the Detroit ghetto, it could have been a dirty word.

"It's the cable car on the other side of the mountain that goes to the top and back."

I congratulated him for focusing on number one, while at the same time keeping his eye on each step of the way. I gave him a gold No. 1 pin. Then I added something that I had not mentioned in my lecture. I told him that in the United States we once had a great baseball player, a pitcher named Satchel Paige, who was reported to have said: "Don't look back. Something might be gaining on you." I disagree. I told that sales manager that it's important to look back, just as he did in mountain climbing or on his job. I told him that I have a framed picture of myself in my office—Joe Girard at the age of nine, shining shoes in a Detroit bar. Underneath is written: "You never want to forget where you came from!"

How Not to Get to the Top

You and I know that many people have reached the top by means that have nothing to do with what this book is all about. You can probably count those people on one hand. We all know the saying, "It's not *what* you know but *who* you know." It's the excuse used most often by people who aren't moving ahead. Don't get me wrong. It's fine to know people in high places, who have clout, who can put in a good word for you, who can help you. That's called networking, and there's nothing wrong with it. But the Girard advice still applies: God and networking do a better job of helping those who help themselves.

I'll bet you know someone who got to the top because he's the boss's nephew or she's the boss's niece. How about the man who got way up there because he married the boss's daughter?

How about being a good old boy and part of a good old boys group? Or a lodge member or fraternity brother? These types often push one another to the top, even when getting there isn't a right that's earned. Nothing beats the success achieved *on your own*.

I can't deny that many people reach the top and attain fame, or at least notoriety, by mastering different steps. Read the supermarket tabloids and you'll discover how some actors and actresses, often without an ounce of talent, made it big with the help of the so-called casting couch. They mattressed their way upward, and often spend years and a lot of money living it down.

Some people rise like cream because they have "connections," or know where the body's buried, or have knifed someone in the back. If you know people like that, broom them out of your life—the sooner the better. You better believe that in the long run, most of those "toppers" won't last. Their methods of reaching success usually don't provide staying power.

Getting There and Staying There

This book not only deals with how to master your way to the top but how to *stay* there. But don't expect that to happen overnight. It takes preparation, knowledge, skills, the ability to set reasonable goals, sound judgment, determination, and continuous self-development. If that sounds like too much to ask, lay this book aside or loan it to a friend, or give it to your Aunt Milly for a doorstop.

If you think it's not too much to ask, congratulations. Know this: The important steps I mastered, and that you too can master, can take you where you want to go, honorably and with a great and satisfying sense of accomplishment.

I share my secrets and some useful strategies for achieving success in business as well as in other walks of life. That's why this is a "how to" book, detailing many important steps and techniques for mastering your way to the top. I've boiled down what I've learned through my own experiences and from what others have told me who have achieved success. I'm grateful to the people who were willing to share their stories with me. Whether they were business or personal successes, their stories are inspirational.

What's in Store

This book covers in detail three important guidelines for reaching the top:

1. Specific steps to be mastered in order to achieve success in business or to reach your personal goals.
2. Examples of how I mastered and applied these steps to my own life and business career as a salesperson, writer, and lecturer.
3. Examples of how other people mastered these steps on their way to the top in their business and professional careers.

Mastering the essential steps puts you in good company: Winston Churchill, prime minister of England and World War II heroic figure; Ronald Reagan, president of the United States; publishers like William Randolph Hearst, with his chain of newspapers, or Adolph Ochs, who rescued the ailing *New York Times* and made it one of the great journals of the world; Sally K. Ride, the first woman astronaut in space; Sandra Day O'Connor, the first woman justice on the U.S. Supreme Court; and great baseball players like Willie Mays, Ty Cobb, and Nolan Ryan. Every one of them—and thousands of people like them—got to the top by mastering most or all of these steps, in one form or another.

Here are some things you'll learn:

- How to get a handle on the top position you want to reach—how to define it and spell it out. You'll be able to see your goal as clearly as if you're viewing it through top-flight binoculars.
- How to visualize your goal, paint a picture of it, frame it, and hang it up in your mind where you can see it every day. That vision will be your own picture, not somebody else's paint-by-numbers goal. I'll guide you, but you'll be the one gripping the handle of the paint brush.
- How to aim high yet set reachable, measurable goals

and objectives. You'll learn the eight important
questions you need to ask yourself about your goals,
and how to come up with the right answers.

- How to challenge yourself, to be daring and take
risks in business and in life, and how living on
the edge can be rewarding.
- How to pump up your confidence muscles without
taking mental steroids—a daily workout that
builds self-assurance and self-esteem.
- How to remember that you're number one, and
how to prove it to yourself every day. You'll get others
to recognize that you're number one and respect
you for it without envy.
- How to keep faith in yourself, in others, and in your
objectives and goals, and maintain your view of
the top, without wavering along the way.
- How to make sure you're the captain of your ship,
no matter how high the waves or how many sharks
in the sea. You'll steer your ship and keep it on
course.
- How to nail down your commitments and keep your
agreements to yourself and to others. Keeping
agreements makes your life work.
- How to practice self-discipline without torturing
yourself. Discipline is an insurance policy for
mastering your way to the top.
- How to consider the company you'll keep along the
way, to know whom you should stay with and whom
you should tell to get lost.
- How to hang in there, to walk a tightrope without
falling, to swim and not sink.
- How to keep enjoying the payoff, and look around
for new "tops" you might want to scale.

Some Important Suggestions

Don't be a speed reader even if you took a high-ticket course in how to become one. Nobody ever got the full flavor, the full meaning of a text by racing through it as if it were the Indy 500. Read this book carefully, all the way through. Digest it. Get the big picture of what mastering your way to the top is all about. Lay it aside for a week, and let it simmer on the back burner of your mind.

Then, take it a chapter at a time. Then, when you feel you're ready, move on to the next chapter.

Study each step and strategy. Learn the "why" of each step as well as the "how." Study the principles and learn how they apply to your situation.

Let me tell you how I mastered these steps and how I keep using them. Let me show you how others mastered the steps and how they keep following these proven principles for success. Examples are often the best teacher. You'll share my track record on the way to making your own. Remember, if I can do it so can you.

As you read of successful strategies and study these examples, do what I always do: Use a yellow felt marking pen to highlight those strategies you think will be of most use to you. After you've read the book once, look through those highlighted items. You won't believe how much you'll get from the book the second time around.

Now, get to work!

2
Dare to Dream

I'M A DREAMER. Aren't we all?

The beginning words of a popular song, but there's a lot more than poetry here. It was the poet Percy Bysshe Shelley, who wrote: ". . . we might be all / We dream . . ." Poets often pinpoint the truth. I believe what Shelley said: Dreams are what make life more meaningful.

There are a great many people who say dreamers are not *doers*. However, I say they're wrong. Often, the bigger the dream, the bigger the accomplishment. The world is full of people who dared to dream big. Their achievements were "tops" that were mastered by *daring to dream*.

Of course, I'm not talking about the dreams that come when you retire for the night. Or, God forbid, nightmares. How about daydreams? No, although Edgar Allan Poe, author of so many famous short stories and poems, once said that those who dream by day are aware of many things missed by those who dream only at night.

Right now, somewhere, someone is dreaming, creating a "top" to shoot for. But dreaming about something and hoping it will fall into your lap is simply wishful thinking. The important thing is to dare to dream big, then take action to make it come true.

Work Smart to Get There

I know of a young lad who is doing exactly that. He's a high school student from my own state, Michigan. He told me that he has sold many things door-to-door—items such as candy bars, dictionaries, jewelry, candles, and canned corn. Daring to dream big, this teenager has employed several of his friends to sell for him. Now he is moving on to sell products as a fund-raising project for schools. What's his dream? To build a career as a quota-busting salesperson. And I'm betting that his dream will come true. He's already mastering his way there. From candles to canned corn to . . . who knows what? Perhaps automobiles, securities, real estate, or electronics.

You can master the important step of *daring to dream* on your way to the top. I did, and I'm going to show you how, positively and effectively. Once you've taken this step and made it work for you, you'll see how many of the other steps build on this one. It's like building blocks, and you stack them one block at a time.

Earlier, I mentioned the song "I'm a Dreamer, Aren't We All?" Another popular song is "With My Eyes Wide Open I'm Dreaming." I call this wide-awake dreaming. I'm wide awake, yes; but to use the step to greatest advantage, I'm wide-awake dreaming but *with my eyes shut.*

Paint Think-Pictures

Psychologists call it *visualization,* but *visualization* is a two-bit word in my vocabulary. Instead, I like to call it *painting think-pictures*. The technique is an effective way to turn a dream into reality. It works in different ways for different needs, and can be effective in helping one lose weight, quit smoking, manage stress, build confidence, or strengthen willpower.

Of course it's not my idea. I simply adapted the technique from a French philosopher named René Descartes, who affirmed the reality of his body to the reasoning of his mind and thoughts. Descartes, often called the father of modern philosophy, expressed his conviction as "I think, therefore I am." I borrowed something else from Descartes, too. Whatever he did in the field of philosophy and in the areas of science and mathematics, he did step by step, one step at a time. I simply added the idea that the elevator was out of order. There were no elevators in his day.

People will tell you that visualization has been around a long time. They're right. But when I tell them that I call the technique painting think-pictures, they say that's been around a long time, too.

Not so. When I say "think" to them, most believe I'm referring to those signs that hang on office walls or in some stores and locker rooms or to various bumper stickers. Remember them? Whenever I see one I chuckle because most of them are clever, but that's about all.

"Think Spring!"
"Think Thin!"
"Think Big!"
"Think Snow!"
"Think Winning!"

Some are purposely misspelled, like "Thimk," to cause a smile, or that twist the meaning, like "Think or Thwim." They're just words. I wonder who makes them up.

Seeing those words isn't enough, however. You need to see beyond the words and think in pictures. Dare to dream, then create the picture. Create in your mind the picture of winning and snowing, being thin and enjoying spring fever, or seeing whatever you dared to dream come true.

You didn't know you could do that, did you?

Try this: Get away by yourself for a few moments. Find an empty office, a room in your home, a corner of the yard, any place where you can relax, be free from interruptions, and close your eyes. Make yourself comfortable—in a chair, or on the floor, or on the grass. Shut your eyes. Now see before you an empty canvas resting on an easel. With your eyes closed, see yourself picking up a small paintbrush, dipping it in oil paints or watercolors. Then dare to dream and paint its picture. Keep your eyes shut and work on your canvas. Scrape away paint if you wish to, start over if you feel you should. Whatever your dream, *Think* it, *see* it, and *be* it.

The Book of Proverbs states, "As he thinketh in his heart, so is he" (23:7). And that predates Descartes by five or six thousand years. In my steps to the top, I express it like this: *As you see yourself in your mind's eye, so you are.*

The principle can be both negative and positive. For example, if you see yourself in a negative light—as a loser, a lard bucket, a failure, a loudmouth, a shrinking violet, a wallflower, or a smart-ass, that's probably what you are. Whoa! It's time to do something about it. Time to make a change. Time to eliminate the negative and accentuate the positive.

Let me tell you of two instances in my life when I did exactly that. I used this principle in a positive manner.

The Think-Picture of My Father

Throughout my younger years, I lived with my dad telling me I would never amount to anything. Now I see that his negative attitude was the cause of my success. Of course, I also realize that my motivation was simply one of "I'll show him!" Getting even is not good motivation, nevertheless I used it. The bitter memory is behind me now and I thank my late father every day for his impact—negative as it was.

When I began selling automobiles in 1963, at the age of thirty-five, I had a lot of self-doubt. After all, I had just come from a failure in the home-building business. More than ever it seemed my old man was right when he said I'd never amount to anything.

Shortly after I started selling cars, I sat down after hours in my office. I relaxed and made myself comfortable, and I was alone as I shut out the world. I closed my eyes, placed a canvas on the easel, and picked up a brush. No one had told me to do this or how to do it. It just seemed like an idea whose time, as they say, had come.

I started a portrait, and the picture was of my dad, not me. I didn't see myself in the picture at all. What I saw was my dad being dead wrong, a scowl on his face and the words "Joey, you'll never amount to anything" on his lips. I concentrated on that picture every day, always seeing in my mind's eye the pleasure of proving him wrong some time in the future. Wrong as the motivation was, I kept that dream of success as a salesperson foremost, and concentrated on that picture of my old man. An amazing thing took place: I started selling cars like wildfire.

You can't go through life with your eyes closed, however. The next thing to do is to turn that mind's eye think-picture into reality. In my case, I put a framed picture of my dad on my office desk. The think-picture had become my *real* picture. I concentrated on it; each day I'd firm up my resolve to "show him."

It worked. Three years later, at age thirty-eight, I hit the top as the world's number one retail salesperson. It suddenly dawned on me that I'd not been selling those hundreds of cars to prospects and owners. I had sold every one of those cars to a picture of my dad.

The Think-Picture of the Pros

Along the way, I broadened my think-picture technique. I began to clip photos from company newsletters and trade magazines of top automotive salespeople for the make of cars I sold—the pros, the record-breakers. I'd tack those pictures to my office wall. This always surprised the people I worked with. I didn't tell them my secret. Instead, when I could be undisturbed, I'd sit down, shut my eyes, pick up that brush again, and start painting. The think-picture was of my beating their sales records, wanting to make sure my mention in the *Guinness Book of Records* remained.

I overtook all the top salespeople, first in the dealership, then in the zone, then in the region, and finally in America and the world. None of those salespeople ever knew that, in my think-picture, I was selling my cars to *them*.

Earlier, I mentioned that there were two instances in my life when I used the think-picture technique of making what I dared to dream come true. The second situation had to do with bulk. Lots of it.

The Think-Picture of a Fatty

Years ago I saw myself as a slob, and was content to remain that way. I was very fat. I am 5'9" tall, and at the time I weighed 207 pounds. I wasn't actually obese, but I was well on my way to being so. For a salesperson, image is very important, and my image wasn't what it should be.

Often, I would be at one end of the showroom in the automobile dealership where I worked. I'd hear a prospect ask another salesperson, "I'm looking for Joe Girard. Where is he?" I didn't like it when I'd hear the fellow salesperson say to the prospect, "Girard's that fat guy over there." I decided to do something about it.

I had to lose fifty pounds of lard. This became a "top" for

me at the time. So, I tried dieting but nothing happened. I bought calorie counters and nothing happened. I purchased a new scale for the bathroom; I'd stand on it and the needle wouldn't move even a fraction of an ounce lower. I exercised—a daily dozen, a daily two dozen. Nothing happened.

Then I got some advice from Jack LaLanne, the physical fitness king whom I had met at a Golden Plate Award banquet. (You'll read about Jack's business success story in Chapter 15.) "So you're the World's Greatest Salesman," he said. He looked me up and down. Then he told me he liked my techniques for professional salesmanship. He also said that from the neck up I was good-looking, but that from the neck down I was ugly and needed to get the blubber off.

He was right, of course, but what hurt was that he said this in front of a room full of people, including my friend the late Lowell Thomas, the world's first radio broadcaster and author of many books. (You'll read about Lowell in Chapter 16.) Jack gave me some exercises and diet tips, and a word of advice. He said that more than diet and exercise is needed. He said it was self-image.

A few days later I looked in the mirror after taking a shower, and I realized that the image I saw was the *real* me and not a picture of the person I wanted to be. I knew that my goal of losing fifty pounds was wishful thinking, that my mental picture had to be one of achievement.

I sat down in a comfortable chair. I relaxed. I was alone and I shut out the world. I closed my eyes, propped a canvas on the easel, and picked up the brush. I started to paint a picture of who I wanted to be and how I wanted to look. Up to that time no doctor had told me to lose weight for health reasons. But Jack LaLanne had been pretty frank when he said I looked ugly from the neck down. My motivation to paint a think-picture was simply that I wanted to look good. I painted a slim, trim, well-muscled Joe Girard. A big dream picture.

As I said earlier, the idea is to dare to dream, but then to *work smart* to make that come true. Every day from then on, first thing in the morning, I'd sit down, close my eyes, and concentrate on the picture of the slim me that I had created. With that picture in my mind's eye, I followed my diet, did my exercises, and everything now began to work in some mysterious way. Once again, the think-picture began to become reality.

I put the think-picture of me into a well-cut, quality suit designed to fit my slim figure. The suit was complemented by a fine shirt and tie, socks and shoes. Everything coordinated. This wardrobe was in sizes smaller than what I wore each day. So, again it was dream into reality. I went shopping and bought a new suit, shirt, tie, socks, and shoes—just like the ones in my think-picture. This wardrobe was several sizes smaller than what I wore. I hung the suit in the closet, then put away the shirt and tie, socks and shoes.

The new clothing was a constant motivation, just as had been the picture of my dad and the photos of pro salesmen as I continued to boost my car sales. Soon I grew nearer to the picture I had painted. I shrank to the suit size, and I've stayed there ever since.

Some people might argue that diet and exercise alone would have done the trick, and that I didn't need to paint think-pictures of my dream figure. Maybe yes, maybe no.

Accentuate the Positive

Remember, dare to dream; and dream big, then make a think-picture of your dream. Paint it in your mind's eye—in Technicolor. Put something important in your think-picture that belongs directly to your dream—an object such as a house, a car or a fleet of cars, a bank, a sailboat, a person other than yourself, or something that is not physical, something no more concrete than an idea.

There is no room in a think-picture for negative images. If

you paint a think-picture of your dream and at the same time consider what if that won't come true, you can be sure that it won't. There is no room for *what ifs* when you dare to dream.

You can bet that Ferdinand de Lesseps never said *what if* the Suez Canal won't hold water? Or Robert Fulton said *what if* my little steamboat blows up? All think-pictures should be positive. Picture being successful. Picture *winning*!

Then always keep that mental picture in mind. In time you can turn the think-picture into reality: a suit or dress in the closet you can't get into yet; the model of a car or small plane you're going to own; a small hedge clipper to keep you focused on the landscaping company you plan to own and operate. Never let your think-picture slip away.

There's a fine line between wishing and dreaming. There's an even bigger line between dreaming and doing. Most people wish upon a star. It's fine and fun, but it doesn't mean a thing unless you follow that star. In other words, *do* something about realizing your dream.

It's fun to build castles in the air, and keep your head in the sky. But it's all a waste of time if you haven't got your feet planted firmly on the ground. When you dare to dream, to visualize or make think-pictures, be sure they are realistic goals for you, and not nonproductive fantasies.

I'm a dreamer. Aren't we all?

3
Know Where You're Going

EVERY GOOD AUTOMOBILE salesperson knows, or should know, the importance of giving a prospect or customer a demonstration ride. If the sales presentation is a good one, the demo is the frosting on the cake. If the sales presentation leaves something to be desired, the demo ride just might make up for it and save the sale.

Car manufacturers and dealers offer all kinds of incentives to get salespeople off their duffs and to motivate them to make sure the prospect gets a demo ride. Dealer advertisements offer all kinds of inducements to come in and test-drive the product. If you're a car salesperson you know what I'm talking about, and if you've been in the market for a new set of wheels you also know what I'm talking about.

Too many salespeople skip the demo ride altogether, saying "Who needs it to make a sale?" A very low percentage of prospects ask for one, although they should. Many salespeople toss the keys to a prospect interested in a car or light truck and say, "Hey, take this baby out for a spin around the block. Try it on for size." The prospect is on his or her own because the salesperson is back in the dealership, hanging around the coffee machine with what I like to call the club, or the bull ring. The prospect gets a ride in the new vehicle all right, but doesn't get a demonstration ride.

Many salespeople do get into the vehicle with a prospect and they head off somewhere so the prospect can enjoy the ride and see how the car handles. After five minutes or so (long enough for the appraiser to insult the prospect's trade-in), they're back in the dealership. I call that half a demonstration ride.

A demo ride worthy of the name is *planned*. The salesperson knows where he or she is going for the ride and where he or she is going for the sale. The salesperson plans carefully the route to include highways, business streets, and residential avenues so that the car is demonstrated in all kinds of traffic conditions, from heavy to light. The salesperson also chooses roads with curves, rough pavement, stop signs, and traffic lights. That way the prospect gets a real feel for the car's power in passing, the way it smooths out rough roads, how it corners, and how it brakes. As part of the planning, a good salesperson changes places with the prospect and lets him or her take the wheel. That's working smart.

Just as knowing where you're going is the key element of a car salesperson's demo ride, so too it's an important step for anyone, in any walk of life, who wants to reach the top.

A Rudderless Ship

Maybe your goal keeps slipping away, looks a bit out of focus, seems shrouded in mist. Maybe you're having trouble getting a handle on it.

Five'll get you ten, you haven't defined your "top"—haven't spelled it out. Could be you've been sailing along with a vague idea about where you want to go—somewhere, someday, somehow. That's like sailing a ship without a rudder. Remember this parent and kid conversation that went something like this:

MOTHER: Where did you go?

KID: Out.

MOTHER: What did you do?

KID: Nothing.

Not very definite, is it? Too many adults, like the kid in this example, play the "going out, doing nothing" game and wonder why their "top" is never quite within reach. *It's because it isn't there!*

When I was a kid growing up in the Detroit ghetto, I remember my mother's singing a song called "Beautiful Isle of Somewhere." She'd get that far-away look in her eyes, and I knew she was dreaming of distant places. I never knew if, in her mind's eye, she ever reached that somewhere isle. I hope she did, but I doubt it.

This I don't doubt: In today's business world, your top—your view of personal success—better have a sharper definition than just "somewhere."

Let's consider the many ways people in all walks of life, business and personal, regard success. Some of the viewpoints can be defined as definite tops. Others are by-products gained when you master your way up the mountain's peak.

How Most Individuals View Success

To many people, success means *money*:

- Lots of it. A huge, fat, cholesterol-rich, weekly, monthly, or yearly income larded with perks and bonuses.
- Earning power that won't quit.
- High-yield investments and blue-chip stocks in a portfolio the size of Delaware.
- Numbered Swiss bank accounts.

- Being able to afford anything your heart desires, including Fort Knox, which holds most of our nation's gold.
- Just enough green stuff to handle any money worries.

Yes, to some people, having money is very important. For example, it can bring *possessions:*

- A handsome colonial/Cape Cod/ranch style home on landscaped acres, or just a cabin in the woods on a lake or river, or in a canyon.
- Impressive furnishings, antiques, art objects.
- A top-of-the-line domestic-make car in the garage (maybe two) and an expensive import in the driveway just for show.
- A speedboat or a yacht, or maybe both at the marina.
- Your own jet, even a prop job, at the local airport.
- A designer wardrobe, expensive genuine jewelry.
- Extensive real estate holdings here and abroad.

To some people, having many possessions is the mark of success. They bring *prestige:*

- Fame, even notoriety, in your field.
- Honors and degrees.
- Recognition wherever you go.
- Invitations to speak before important groups.
- Being sought after for one social function after another.
- Being a hero, whether in sports, in the military, or to your kid.

To some people, having a name that's known and admired everywhere is all that matters. It means *control:*

- Owning your own business, being in charge, and enjoying the independence.
- Being a manager, a supervisor, a foreman, a union shop steward, a purchasing agent, a senior editor.
- Being a coach, a referee, a scoutmaster, or an umpire who calls the shots on the playing fields of life.

For many people, being in control of things is the chief measure of success. These examples of the way many people regard the top are showy things.

There's Nothing Wrong with the Good Things in Life

There's nothing wrong with having money. I'm sure you like having it; so do I. Remember the song in the stage musical and movie *Fiddler on the Roof*? We've all sung it to ourselves and without shame: "If I Were a Rich Man." We get a kick out of listing all the things we'd do if we were rich.

When I was a kid, my family was dirt poor. Of course, I didn't know it then because my mother was a genius at making both ends meet with the money my dad and I managed to earn.

As a shoe-shine boy, not yet a teenager and working the bars and saloons of Detroit, Michigan, I didn't earn very much, yet every bit counted. I worked smart even then. I could snap a tight rag over a pair of shoes with the best of them. Still, like most kids, I liked to sneak off to have some fun. My old man didn't like that. He was all work and no play. As I told you earlier, he put me down, over and over.

"Joey, you're a bum, you're a zero. You'll never amount to

anything. You like to have fun too much. You'll never make any money. You'll always be a bum!"

I think the reason my dad said it so often was that he didn't think I believed—as he did—that money was the greatest thing since Sicilian pizza. He was wrong. I knew even then that money made the world go 'round. I knew that I was needed to help out at home, so I hustled to make a dollar—and still had fun where I could find it.

Now, when I speak before large groups of salespeople, managers, and directors, I tell them that story. I describe how my dad was absolutely right—I've proved him to be right. Work isn't the beginning and end of everything; I still like to have fun. I still like to play. I'm still a bum. Then I add, "but I'm a *rich* bum!"

There's nothing wrong with earning and having lots of money. Remember that the scriptures say it's the *love* of money—not money itself—that's the root of all evil.

Possessions? Why not have them. I'm sure you enjoy the ones you have; so do I. I like my house, its furnishings, my cars, and my motor home. I enjoyed the cabin cruiser I owned until the family got seasick. Good-bye cruiser!

I like the den that I've filled with items I've collected on business and pleasure trips all over the world: a fifty-year-old working jukebox, Tiffany lamps, autographed photographs, slot machines, a real barber chair and barber pole, musical instruments, a mounted blue marlin, and license plates from everywhere. When you think of the possessions you now own or the ones you hope to own—or when you're envying others for what they have—remember that the scriptures also warn that where your treasure is, there your heart is also.

Make sure that as you master your way to the top, *you* own your possessions and they don't own you. For example, a friend of mine is afraid to travel. He fears that when he's gone, someone will steal his original oil paintings, his expensive stereo system, his large-screen projection television, his several high-tech VCRs, his huge collection of current and classic films on videotape, his many compact discs, and his thousand-volume library with first editions (the prized ones being by Nathaniel Hawthorne, the nineteenth-century author of *The Scarlet Letter*). All his material possessions are covered by insurance; of course, many of them are irreplaceable. I can understand why my friend worries. My friend firmly believes he owns many valuable things. But does he? Or do the possessions own him? You better believe it.

Prestige? It's nice to have and there's nothing wrong with it. We all admired General "Stormin' Norman" Schwarzkopf of the Persian Gulf War, just as in the past we admired generals like Dwight D. Eisenhower and Douglas MacArthur of World War II fame. We're proud of ballplayers like Orel Hershiser today just as we hailed Mickey Mantle and Roger Maris in the past. People think Robert Redford and Kevin Costner are the screen greats of today, as were Clark Gable and Gary Cooper in years gone by. Madonna counts fans in the millions, but Marilyn Monroe had even greater fame in her career. Prestige has always been highly prized.

It's natural to want to be well thought of. I'm sure you enjoy the feeling. So do I. When the late Dr. Norman Vincent Peale, author of *The Power of Positive Thinking*, wrote the foreword to my book *How to Sell Yourself*, he lent some of his prestige to me, and I've always been grateful for it—especially when he said, "Joe Girard can help you. I know because he helped me."

I like being booked to give lectures and seminars. I'm pleased when people ask me to autograph my books. I enjoy being in the *Guinness Book of Records*. When you've mastered your way to the top you find that you've earned a measure of prestige. That's fine, as long as you keep a level head about it—which means not letting it go to your head. When it becomes an ego trip and success goes to your head, you know what they say: The old hat doesn't fit anymore.

There's a lot of satisfaction in having your name recognized.

Somebody once said that a man's name should appear in a newspaper only twice in his lifetime: when he's born and when he dies. Don't believe it. If your name is free from scandal or gossip, if it reflects worthy accomplishments, then enjoy the prestige.

Less Is Often More

Money, possessions, prestige—all are fine. They are symbols of success. But money, possessions, prestige, and control are not that meaningful to some individuals. For many other people there are less flashy marks of success, and they are just as fine as the one's we've covered:

- Raising a well-adjusted family whose members are law-abiding, productive members of society.
- Earning a scholarship and going to college, getting a degree, or simply going back to finish high school.
- Being a credit to your community and active in service to it, whether in local civic affairs, your church, or volunteering to do something when someone is needed to do it.
- Planning for retirement, enjoying retirement, and taking time to smell the roses when you get there.
- Enjoying good health, being heart-smart, diet-conscious, exercising, and following the advice of your doctor.

That last one is a must in my book. I make sure I have an annual physical, work out in my own fitness room, and there's a lot less of me around the waist than there was a few years ago. Your goal might very well be to get in shape. A healthy body, not necessarily a show-off body, spells success in my book. You'd be surprised at the number of businesses that provide exercise facilities for their employees. They've found out that working out means not only working better but working smart.

As you can see, people's viewpoints about success differ. I know one businessman who would rather have "Vice President" on his office door than have a raise. That was his top. He mastered his way there and he was happy.

Opening the world to a pupil or a classroom of students may be all the success wished for by a dedicated, but often underpaid teacher. I bet you know one or two such teachers. Preservation of our forests, cleanup of our lakes and rivers, and air free from pollution are successes that conservationists strive for.

A breakthrough in medical research—discovering a cure for cancer or saving human lives through a transplant may be the greatest success that can be attained. Here, business know-how is as important as medical know-how, because the costs can be in megabucks.

There are all kinds of "tops," aren't there? That's why it's so important to define the top you're trying to reach, to narrow the field, to know *absolutely* where you're going.

Know Exactly Where You're Going

Do you like riddles? I do. This is one of my favorites and I guess it's as old as time.

> As I was going to St. Ives,
> I met a man with seven wives,
> Each wife had seven sacks,
> Each sack had seven cats,
> Each cat had seven kits:
> Kits, cats, sacks, and wives,
> How many were there going to St. Ives?

Many people try to answer the question by counting all the "sevens." Since you are working smart from now on, you're not going to bother to count. You know there was only one person going to St. Ives. The narrator obviously knew where he was going.

The unasked and unanswered question is *why*? What did he expect to achieve when he got to St. Ives? Was it part of a top for him? All we can say about that person is that he knew where he was going. That much is to his credit.

You'd be surprised at the number of people in all walks of life, in all lines of business, who have no idea where they're going. I don't mean where they're going down the street, or to their jobs, or to their homes, or to the beach, or to the ball-park, or local pool hall for a game of snooker. I mean where they're going in their work and where they're going in their lives. If they can't answer to where they're going, what top they want to achieve, they'll never master their way there. Unlike some rudderless humans, you're going to know where you're going.

After my talks, I sometimes ask people—or stop friends and business associates, or ask a waiter or waitress—this question: Where are you going in your career—in your life? Do you dare to dream? Where is your dream taking you?

I get strange looks. I hear a foreign language, and I don't mean French or German or Italian or Polish, although that sometimes happens. I hear: "*Uh, um, umph, ah, stimpf, yeah, zirt, xnth, uh, scrample,*" which translates to "I honestly don't know where I'm going."

Heading for Nowheresville

Where do you want to go? *Somewhere*. Even if you don't know where you're going, you're going to wind up somewhere. I call it nowheresville. And that's no place to be.

Only you can decide what top you wish to reach. You must decide it, define it, nail it down, tie it up, keep it in plain sight, before you can take the steps to reach it. I can't pick your top for you, but I can show you some important steps to help you get there. One such step is *to make sure you know where you're going*. Real sure.

Think carefully, then ask yourself: What do I want at my job, in my business, in my career, at school or college, in my marriage, in my life, so badly that I can taste it? I've asked that question many times in my life, especially when I have come face-to-face with a career change. If you want something so badly you can taste it, you want to make sure it leaves a pleasant taste, not a sour one.

As a businessman I wanted success as a builder of homes. I could taste it; what I got was the sour taste of failure. Then I wanted success as a salesperson—so bad I could taste it. What I got was a pleasant taste of success—something to smile about.

How did I learn about the taste test? Near where I grew up is a Capuchin monastery. I've known the friars for years. Father Solanus, a humble priest back then and a candidate for sainthood now, kept me out of reform school and taught me that knowing *exactly* what I was wishing for was far different from wishful thinking. I've never forgotten his words. You may not have a Capuchin monastery near you, so I'll let you borrow mine, as well as the good advice of Father Solanus.

One Christmas eve years ago he said to me, "Be careful about what you wish for, Joe. You just might get it!" I was puzzled. It seemed to me that if I got what I wished for, I'd be very happy. It took me a while to realize what he meant. A wish might come true, but a wrong wish fulfilled can lead straight to nowheresville.

So, know *for sure* where you're going. Define your top, then take the right steps to get there. Don't *wish* to get to the top. Wishing, hoping, yearning, aching, trusting will never get you there.

Years later, as a failed builder, I realized I had not known where I really was going. I remembered the good priest's words, and my new resolve marked a turning point in my life.

I have a sign on my office wall that reads:

> The secret of life is to *know* what you want, *write* it
> down, then *commit yourself* to accomplishing it.

Not only do I have those words on my office wall but I also have them on the sun visor of my car.

Another caution: Master your way to the top in the field you've chosen, then start your way up in another field, if that's your desire. If you try to reach too many tops at the same time, you'll wind up only spinning your wheels.

The Right to Change Direction

Does all this mean you can't change your mind about your top? Of course not. Can you switch from one top, once you've reached it, to another? Of course you can.

In my hometown, Henry Ford was a successful watchmaker, a career in itself in his day. But he shifted gears and became the most successful automobile manufacturer in the world— and Detroit put the world on wheels.

The Wright brothers were doing just fine as builders of bicycles and owners of an Ohio bicycle shop. They pedaled hard and fast until their wheels took wings, and they gave the world the aeroplane.

People everywhere go from one top to another. In my case it was from selling to lecturing to writing. Later, I'll tell you how a leading hair stylist changed his top. He now owns a multimillion-dollar distributorship in hair products. It's a success story that will knock your socks off.

I'll also tell you how a man I know went from bottling his own spaghetti sauce—no, it's not Paul Newman—to developing a multimillion-dollar food business. Each of these people mastered their way to the top, and I've made their way part of the steps discussed in this book.

4
Set Goals for Success

W HEN I WAS a teenager the word *goal* meant only one thing: getting a touchdown. The streets and alleys of Detroit were our playing fields. They were pretty rough gridirons, and my friends and I never used fancy terms like "goal to go." We didn't have wide receivers or tight ends. Every game was a scrimmage that started with the snap of the ball and usually ended in a fight. A neighborhood kid owned the football, and when he picked it up to go home or when the streetlights came on, the game was over.

We never had a game plan more complicated than that. We knew only that the game meant making a goal. But as an adult, reaching a desired goal calls for a very definite game plan. Without a plan you'll have a difficult time getting to your goal. Life has a way of putting obstacles in your path, so it takes a game plan of steps and strategies to knock them down successfully.

Take hockey, for example. There's a goalie out in front to protect the net. Just ask Wayne Gretzky, top National Hockey League scorer, who melted the ice for the Edmonton Oilers and now the Los Angeles Kings, what it takes to smash the puck past the goalie. In soccer, ask Pelé, recognized as the greatest soccer player in the world. The Brazilian scored over 1,000 goals simply by kicking the ball where it belongs, as if the goalie weren't there.

You master your way to the top by setting goals along the way and going after them as if there weren't a goalie to stop you. I know a boat salesman whose showroom is right next to a marina on Lake St. Clair, which is just a stone's throw from where I live. He's an only kid and is still single. He says that when obstacles or goalies get in the way of his goals, he simply goes after them until they cry uncle. "Since I haven't any nieces and nephews," he says, "it's the only way I can feel I'm an uncle." It works for him and that's all that matters.

Setting goals is an important step as you head for the top. In your overall game plan, break this step down into a number of smaller steps. It doesn't matter what your business is—or your profession, or your job, or whatever the top is you're going for; the principles and strategies for setting goals and achieving them are the same.

My "49" Sign

Here's what I mean by breaking down a goal into smaller steps. For many years I had a sign on a wall in my office in the car dealership where I worked. It read "49." That's all.

Fellow salespeople, dealership brass, customers, and prospects would look at it, stare a bit, then always ask: "Joe, what's with this '49'?" I'd smile, say nothing, and keep them guessing. It was my personal secret. Actually, that "49" was a constant reminder of the two main goals I had set for myself in life.

On Christmas eve of 1977 I called a press conference. That's a fancy way to say that a few local reporters jammed into my office, who knew of my track record as a retail salesperson. A couple of the reporters asked, "Joe, what does '49' mean?"

"I'm forty-nine years old," I said, "and that sign was to

remind me of a major goal—one of two—that I set for myself a few years back."

"What were they?" they asked.

"The first was to quit my sales career at age forty-nine. I've reached that goal this year. It took a lot of steps to get to that top." On my office wall I had a calendar, and each month as I tore off that page, I'd look at my "49" sign and say, "We're getting closer, Joey, to leaving here and showing others how to reach their goals."

The reporters would then ask, "Doing what? Showing others how to sell?"

"Maybe. But not just that. Showing others how to reach the top. The top may be different for different people, but the steps for mastering your way there are the same."

"So that's your second goal? Teaching others?" one would ask.

"In time, maybe. No, my second goal is quite different."

I remember spreading open a catalog showing many models of motor homes—handsome, streamlined, a home away from home. "All my adult life I dreamed of having a motor home. It was something I dared to visualize when the prospects of ever having one seemed pretty dim. No matter. I've always dreamed big. I made the dream a goal. At last I've reached that goal." As I set out to attain it, I knew that I would have to break that goal down into a series of little goals—smaller steps—if I were to see it become a reality.

Years ago I'd get a station wagon from the dealership and load it with picnic baskets, blankets, folding chairs—everything to make a getaway day in the outdoors a pleasant experience. Our "home away from home" was a nearby park, a beach, or a place miles into the country.

"One day," I promised my wife, June, "we'll have a motor home."

Then we graduated to a tent, our family's first real "home away from home." We went camping, pitching our tent at state parks or just somewhere off the beaten path. We had cots, air mattresses, sleeping bags, a portable gasoline stove, an ice chest, and a battery-operated radio with which to catch the Detroit Tigers ball game. We also had mosquitoes, snakes, raccoons, and porcupines.

"One day, June, we'll have a motor home. I promise. When I'm forty-nine. Look forward to it, look to the day." Well, that day came. Unfortunately my wife passed away before she could enjoy the motor home I'd promised. However, she was uppermost in my mind as I set out finally to achieve the goal.

I mentioned in my book *How to Close Every Sale* that I considered the Airstream the Rolls-Royce of motor homes. It was Larry Huttle, now president of Airstream, who convinced me that I should buy an Airstream. I did. In fact, I owned several Airstreams. I admired not only the models but also the corporation's sales and marketing strategies. And I found an excellent way to help them market their product.

I sat down with Larry Huttle and came right to the point. "How would you like to have me as a spokesperson for Airstream? I'll be in your advertisements in recreational vehicle magazines. I'll appear twice a year at your sales or other meetings and share my strategies for business success with your RV representatives."

He grinned. "How much of the factory do you want me to hand over?"

"None of it. All I'd like is an Airstream Motor Home, top of the line and updated every year."

"Sold!"

I've been with Airstream ever since. I've traveled all over North America in what I now call my "wheel estate"—a rolling home away from home with unbeatable comfort; great sleeping, cooking, and dining facilities; and television.

The talked-about sign, "49," helped me keep those two goals always in mind—one a business goal and the other a personal goal.

Eight Important Questions

Whatever goal you set for yourself, you must consider it from a number of angles. Write down your goal and then ask yourself these eight questions:

1. Have I clearly defined my goal? Have I spelled it out?
2. Is it a minor or a major goal? How important is it?
3. Is my goal a long-range one, a short-range one, or both?
4. Is it a realistic goal? Or is it wishful thinking?
5. Is it an achievable goal for me? Am I up to it?
6. As I strive to reach the goal, can I measure my progress so I can know if I'm winning?
7. Is my goal flexible so it can change when my needs change?
8. What sacrifices are required in time, energy, and money?

So much for the questions. They could be rephrased in a number of ways, but coming up with the answers is not always easy. Let's consider how some or all of these eight questions impact on some typical goals.

Suppose your goal is to quit smoking. You can define it by stating simply "I'm quitting the weed, period." To some people this is a minor goal, simply a bad habit to be got rid of. To others it may be a major goal because of doctor's orders. (That was the situation in which I found myself. I was smoking three and a half packs a day.) Or it may be a major goal for people who take the Surgeon General's warnings seriously. The goal can also be long-range (tapering off gradually) or short-range (quitting cold turkey).

Today, with so many health studies linking smoking to diseases such as cancer, heart trouble, and strokes, quitting certainly is a desirable goal. Is it an achievable goal for you? Maybe yes, maybe no. We all know people who say, "I've tried quitting for twenty or more years with no luck." We also know that luck has nothing to do with it. You can measure progress if the method for quitting is to taper off (ten cigarettes today, nine tomorrow, eight the next day, etc.). There is little or no flexibility in this goal, and there are no sacrifices. (Actually you're gaining something—better health—and you're saving money too.)

In this way you work through the eight questions to arrive at meaningful answers. You may come to the conclusion that the goal is a realistic one for you, attainable within either long- or short-term limits, and decide to go for it. Other times you may realize that the goal which at first seemed worthwhile is not, so you set your sights on a different goal.

Now let's consider a business goal: becoming a successful broker. If you have worked for some years and/or are now working in a financial organization—a bank or savings and loan institution; a corporation that sells stocks, bonds, and other securities; or a credit union—you can probably supply positive answers to the eight questions. The odds are high that you can reach your goal because you probably have the financial background and the necessary experience, as well as knowledge of what's involved in trading shares. You could move into the investment field and probably achieve success as a broker.

On the contrary, you may have no financial background at all, were never on the working side of the teller's window at your bank, and may never have applied for a loan or mortgage. Perhaps you work at a travel agency and you rent your apartment, or maybe you're a dentist with a thriving practice and you paid cash for your condo. However, you may have invested heavily and regularly in the market, and you may have a portfolio of blue-chip stocks. You're familiar with words and phrases like *stock options, preferred stocks, commodities* and *futures,* and "buying on margin." You take your gains and losses in stride, and love it when there's a stock split. Or, maybe you simply have invested in mutual funds or tax-free municipal bonds.

Would you have a good chance of becoming a successful licensed broker? It's possible, of course. But is it probable? That depends on how you answer the eight questions. Will it demand sacrifice? Yes. You will have to spend time and money learning the investment business from the ground up, and get a job in a brokerage house to move up to a point where you are on your own.

Whether or not you need to answer all eight questions depends on the goal you've defined for yourself. The simpler the answers, the more likely the goal can be achieved. Some goals allow you no flexibility. A rigid goal is difficult to reach when time and circumstances change. For example, suppose your goal is to become advertising manager of your firm. It is a position built into the organizational chart of the company. The job description is clear-cut, written by an outside management group hired by your firm. The position cannot be revised until a three-year study is completed of advertising results versus costs.

You have seniority in the department, and prior employment with a national advertising agency gave you a wealth of experience in the field. Compared to the job description, you are overqualified. A man with lesser experience is hired from the outside. Your goal has suddenly become unreachable because there was no flexibility in the job description.

The situation I've just described happened to a friend of mine, a former automobile customer who worked in a company which manufactured O-rings and gaskets for industrial use and which handled its own advertising. My friend quit, went to another company that put out a similar product, and set a new goal. The new goal was to induce management to handle its own advertising. He compared internal costs with the advertising costs of the agency that the firm used—creative thinking, production costs, media costs, agency markup. He sold management on the idea of "rolling your own." He created the department and automatically became the advertising manager. He worked smart.

Some goals require little sacrifice; others ask for a great deal. One sacrifice my advertising manager friend had to make was to move to another town. He had a home to sell, a home to buy, new schools for his kids, and a less desirable climate.

Objectives and Reality

There are two important principles involving goals that I have followed throughout my life. They're not new, but I've adapted them to fit my wants and needs in business and personal affairs:

1. *Set Objectives.* Break your main goal into smaller ones called objectives, and attain one objective before moving on to the next.
2. *Get Real.* Goals that are unrealistic, far out, or wishful thinking are hard—if not impossible—to achieve.

Consider your *objectives*. This helps you avoid what I call "goal indigestion." Too much of something at one time—too many top goals, for example—can lead to "goal heartburn," if not downright indigestion. You don't want to wind up like that guy in the TV commercial for Alka-Seltzer who kept saying, "I can't believe I ate the whole thing."

Take your goals in nibbles. Always keep your eye on your main goal, but—as I always caution—take a step at a time to get there. Remember, the elevator is out of order. Each step to your main goal can be called an objective. Master it, then move on to the next: an objective here, a pause, an objective there, another pause. Objectives, or "little goals," are a lot easier to achieve on your way to the top than going at once for the big enchilada.

For example, let's say you work in a factory—a manufacturing plant of some kind. It doesn't matter what the product is or what the department might be within the plant. Let's assume you have a goal to be in a managerial position in that factory. In fact, in time you may even set a higher goal—that of plant manager.

If you've answered the eight questions to your satisfaction, particularly the one about defining your goal ("I want to be a department manager and in time the plant manager—a long-range goal"), you must now break it down into a series of smaller objectives while keeping an eye on your main goal.

Each of your objectives—some short-range, some long-range—must also test against the eight questions and answers. That done, your objectives might shape up like this: Seek to be a straw boss or crew chief, then shoot for foreman, then go for supervisor or similar position in your department, then set your sights on department head. Soon you may find yourself well on your way to becoming plant manager. Seem impossible? Many a plant manager in the United States can tell you that's how they got to the top. The U.S. industrialist Andrew Carnegie started out as a young dollar-a-week laborer in a cotton factory. His goals, his daring to dream big, always led him to greater achievements. He moved from factory to railroads, from telegraph operator for the Pennsylvania Railroad to superintendent. Always eager, always moving on, he left railroads for iron and steel. He brought the Bessemer process for making steel to the United States. Finally, the U.S. Steel Company grew as a corporate giant because of Carnegie's goal achievements. Legend has it that as a boy he used to sweep the floors of the place he worked; if true, his achievements are all the more remarkable.

Who says it can't be done again? In fact, that's what America is all about. The step-at-a-time principle—small objectives along the way to the top—holds true for whatever major goal you desire.

Now let's consider the second principle, *get real*. Many people fail to reach their goals because the goals are unrealistic. They don't fit the pattern of the person defining the goal. For example, suppose a worker in a city's wastewater treatment plant decides he wants to become an account executive in an advertising agency. It's not absolutely impossible, of course, but a more realistic goal—a more achievable one—would be to secure a position on the city's or county's water board.

To be realistic, your goals should be in line with:

- Your background, work-related or personal
- Your level of experience, now and in the past
- Your current and past responsibilities at work
- Your monetary worth and cash flow (although that is not always a factor)
- Your education
- Your physical condition or health

Some or all of those factors contribute to the realism of a goal. There are always exceptions to the rule. For example, at one time my goal was to sell more vehicles at retail in the dealership than any other salesperson there. Was the goal realistic? For me, yes, even though I had no background or experience in selling cars, had no "cash flow," and most of my education was from the school of hard knocks (I am literally self-educated). But I had going for me at the time a good physical condition (a plus derived from growing up in the Detroit ghetto), which helped me endure the long hours involved in prospecting and selling to reach my goal. Still, the *get real* principle should be part of your goal-setting procedures. The more realistic your objectives and main goal, the more likely you are to achieve them.

Goal-Oriented People

Take the time to read about people in all walks of life who have achieved noteworthy goals, whether in business, education, religion, or professions such as law and medicine, and certainly in sports. (Most men and a lot of women are probably more aware of sports figures than successful people in other fields.) Whatever the field, be assured that most of these people achieved their goals over time, a step at a time. Whatever the term used, these "little goals" or objectives played an important part in their achieving the main goals.

5
Be a Risk-Taker

I RECEIVED A LETTER recently from a man in his early thirties in Ontario, Canada. He told me of a step he had taken that involved a great measure of risk: He left the Order of St. Augustine. Now, as a defrocked Roman Catholic priest, he has stepped forth—you might say he was thrust—into an unsheltered, probably hostile world. He has felt vulnerable since the day he left the holy orders. His philosophy, however, has centered around the old saying, "Nothing ventured, nothing gained."

At the time of his letter, the man was about to tackle the business world, with no business experience whatsoever. He did not mention the type of business venture he was interested in. But he had read my book *How to Sell Yourself*, and said it had given him confidence.

Every step that man will take in his new career will probably involve some risk. He is willing to take risks. From the determination he expressed in his letter, I'll bet on his making it in his new world.

Why Put Yourself at Risk?

We put ourselves at risk every waking (and sometimes sleeping) moment of the day. If we didn't, we'd stay rooted in one spot forever. Indeed, when the result of our risk-taking is not to our liking, we use the expression, "I should have stayed in bed."

Many people seem to "stay in bed" all their lives because they do not take any risks in their lives, personal or professional. Yet when we cross the street we risk being hit by a car, a motorcycle, a bus, or a taxi. When we swim in the ocean, we risk being dragged under by an undertow or rip current. Although statistics prove that air travel is safer than auto travel, we place ourselves at risk every time we fly. After all, we must rely on the structural soundness of the aircraft and, if we're not piloting the plane, we must put our trust in the pilot and plane crew. Travel anywhere involves some risk. It can be as minor as losing one's luggage or as major as winding up a hostage in some remote corner of the world.

Risk-taking has been with us as long as recorded history. A volcano buries the towns on its mountainside in ash, but the people go right back "living on the edge," rebuilding their villages. Floods wash away homes and possessions, but when the waters recede, the people clean up the mess and get on with living. Hurricanes, earthquakes, typhoons, tornadoes, landslides, and other natural occurrences do not deter people from facing the same dangers over and over.

An old saying is "Without risk, life has no meaning." It's as true as "If one has not known sadness, he cannot know happiness." Actually we put ourselves in a great many risky situations because we have no choice in the matter. We must cross a street to get to the other side. We must drive a car, take a plane, board a bus, or launch a boat to get from one place to another. But there is a great difference in taking a *calculated risk* and a *foolish risk*.

Calculated Risks vs. Foolish Risks

Being a risk-taker in business—in mastering your way to the top—calls for knowing the difference between the two types of risk. When an individual bungee jumps—that is, jumps off a bridge or a building with nothing but a long "rubber band" to break the fall—that is a foolish risk, despite what those people say who like to do it. The same with skydiving or going over Niagara Falls in a barrel. Or hurtling over a great number of cars, placed side by side, on a motorcycle. All of those acts are foolish risks done by daredevils who live on the edge—although I know daredevils will not agree with me. Nor will tightrope walkers or high-trapeze artists in a circus. And free and easy, promiscuous sex has always been a risk, only more so today.

What, then, are calculated risks? They are deciding to head for the boss's office and ask for a raise. You may or may not get the raise, but at least—as that young, former priest wrote—"nothing ventured, nothing gained."

Changing from a well-paying job to one at lesser pay because the future looks brighter is also a calculated risk. The person who does so may or may not find the new job has a better future. He or she may regret leaving the former position. Yet the fact remains that the person will never know if there is a brighter future unless the risk is taken.

Some people consider marriage a calculated risk. Their attitude often is this: If it doesn't work out, we can always get a divorce.

You know, of course, that I'm not talking about living dangerously, or being reckless, or taking chances. I'm not the wisest of men, but neither am I foolhardy. I expect I'm as cautious as the next. So I'm not advocating that you "go for broke" as you master your way to the top. Getting anywhere at your job or profession—in fact, getting anywhere in life—means you have to take calculated risks. Carefully considered risks. Risks in which you must balance the payoff against the costs in time, money, energy, and other sacrifices or compromises called for.

When you don't take a carefully considered risk you remain where you are. You don't go backward, but you don't go forward, either. You likely remain in some kind of vegetable state.

My Own Calculated Risks

I have taken many risks as I mastered my way to the top. I took a calculated risk when I decided to sell automobiles instead of remaining in the home-building business. I took a calculated risk when I retired from selling cars and turned my energy toward showing others the techniques that could help them get to the top. I took a calculated risk the first time I spoke before a non-English speaking audience, worrying if the translater, communicating to an audience wearing earphones, would be able to interpret the American slang and figures of speech. But if I hadn't taken any of those risks I would still be sitting up to my mortgage in a building career that was going nowhere. Remember, I call it nowheresville.

At one time in my life my family was literally down to its last bag of groceries. Creditors were not just knocking at my door, they were pounding on it. I had wasted time on an unrealistic goal and had lost my shirt; I certainly didn't want to lose my pants as well. So, with nothing to back me but my own determination, I went to work selling cars. No one gave me any encouragement. I had to take the calculated risk of stepping into new territory where I might find either solid ground or quicksand. But I took the risk, watching where I stepped. And I stepped on the egos of envious salespeople as I began to break automobile retail-sales records.

What I learned from that and later experiences is that often one has to skate on thin ice to achieve one's goals and objectives. You, too, will certainly risk thin ice as you master your way to the top. When it comes to thin ice, the gutless refuse to put on skates. But that's not you. You'll put on the skates, size up the situation, and move forward with caution.

Pioneer Risk-Takers

When it comes to risk-taking, I often cite the example of Jamison Handy, a true pioneer in industry and sports. Handy was always willing to take a risk, even though friends and associates frequently warned him about "sticking his neck out." He took risks that challenged his physical courage. He also took risks to test the courage of his convictions.

I was intimately acquainted with his industry record in the field of communications, since he was the genius behind all the training given to sales and service personnel in the dealerships—United States and Canada—that sold the make of cars I represented. Every Monday morning I was exposed to his training materials in sales meetings.

Similarly, generations of schoolchildren have benefited from his educational films. And thousands of members of the armed forces learned military and other skills from Jam Handy films. He believed, as the Chinese philosopher Confucius was supposed to have said, that a picture is worth a thousand words. He felt that teaching, instructing, and training, such as they were, had far too much text and too little illustration.

Handy was a friend of Thomas Edison, inventor of the motion picture. Borrowing the idea of a movie's reel of film, he conceived the idea of putting pictures on a strip of film that could be moved forward a frame at a time. This allowed the teacher or instructor to amplify the ideas the pictures expressed.

Later, he synchronized the pictures to records, creating a true audiovisual medium.

What has this to do with risk-taking? Handy could easily have followed in his father's footsteps in the newspaper business in Chicago, and he would have had the security of a steady job as a journalist. He was considered foolish to give up a sure thing. At the time people were caught up in the magic of silent motion pictures, and friends told him that people would no longer sit still for pictures that didn't move, that only slid forward one at a time. He would be sure to fail. Handy's answer was, "I'll take the risk."

Today, Jam Handy is considered the father of audiovisual training. Risking the courage of his convictions, he developed methods that have trained people in business and industry, in social and civic organizations, in unions and at military installations.

I hail Handy as a risk-taker in another field as well. In his lifetime he was as at home in the water as on the land. A member of two U.S. Olympic swimming teams twenty years apart, he also was winner three times, consecutively, of the National ten-mile Mississippi River Marathon. He swam almost every day of his life, in pools across the country and in both oceans. Winning was in his blood, and he was obsessed with speed. He decided to show swimmers something different.

When he told the champion swimmer Johnny Weissmuller his idea, Weissmuller scoffed. Too big a risk in the water. Besides, the Australian crawl was well-established; you can't change it. Champion swimmer Duke Kahanamobu warned him that he might drown doing what Handy liked to do best. His reply to both his swimming pals was, "I'll take the risk."

Again Handy put the courage of his convictions to the test. He freed the crawl from the way it had been performed in the past. He swam keeping his head down, turning his face to one side to take a breath, then letting that breath out while his face was back in the water. What happened? His speed increased with every stroke. Of course he didn't drown. The risk he took in defying the standard way resulted in the American crawl, seen in every pool around the world. It put him in the International Swimming Hall of Fame.

Jam Handy is now known as the father of modern swimming as well as the father of audiovisual training. And what about the risk-taking that tested his physical courage? It also happened to involve water.

At one time, Jamison Handy took a group of military VIPs on his yacht for a cruise on Chesapeake Bay, to entertain them and to cement some defense training contracts. A tremendous storm developed. Waves grew mountainous. Some of the army and navy brass got seasick. The boat tossed like a cork on the water. As I heard the story, even the helmsman was hanging over the rail.

Handy respected the water, but by nature he had no fear of it. He had no problem risking his will against the storm. He grabbed the wheel. A friend on board, seasick as the others, gasped and said, "You'll never make it." Handy grinned and said he'd take the risk. And doing so, he brought the boat safely into port. Perhaps the story is legendary, but Handy was, as they say, a legend in his own time.

A foolish risk? Perhaps. He might have wound up swimming, perhaps for the last time, in the storm-tossed bay. From then on, Handy was often called "Old G.G.G.," meaning the *Guy's Got Guts*. The point is, to be a risk-taker you've got to have guts and strength of conviction.

Positive Risk-Takers

We have all read about the people who take foolish risks—the daredevils, the sensation seekers. Their exploits fill the news. However, people who take calculated, considered risks in their professions or jobs or schooling—or just everyday living—are just as noteworthy—perhaps even more so. There have been many people who, in the past, were certainly risk-takers in the positive sense: Howard Hughes, the industrialist, perfected oil-drilling tools. Walt Disney believed he could interest adults and children in animated cartoons, just as they were interested in regular films. President Thomas Jefferson took a big risk in buying the Louisiana Territory from the French for $15 million at a time when the U. S. Treasury was not exactly bursting at the seams. William Seward, secretary of state in President Abraham Lincoln's cabinet, took a tremendous calculated risk when he purchased Alaska from the Russians for $7 million. The risk paid off, but at the time the naysayers called it "Seward's Folly."

Just as the past is full of risk-takers, so too is today. At the moment you're reading this book, thousands of people are taking the risks involved to reach the top in their jobs and professions, and are enriching their lives with new and rewarding experiences.

The Need for Courage

You need courage to be a risk-taker. Remember the example of the *Guy's Got Guts*? One important way to keep your courage up is not to let others—the naysayers—discourage you. You'll always find wet blankets to warn you about taking risks. Have the courage to go for the top, to go for success. It takes guts to do so.

Many people are afraid of success. They're afraid of what success might bring. They say, "If I get to the top I'll be responsible for my employees." Or "People will be jealous of me and will probably hate me or stab me in the back." Or "If I earn the kind of money I want to make, I'll just have to pay more taxes." And on and on.

You may never have thought that some people are afraid to master their way to the top. They are people who, as kids, played the game King of the Hill. They remember that when they were King, the other kids wanted to knock them off. But when that happened, they took a risk and got the hill back. Many adults need to develop the same courage they had as kids, but calculating carefully how to get "their hill, their top," not by pushing and shoving recklessly to gain the hill.

It's all right to have a bit of "kid courage" in you. Consider the baseball player, Ricky Henderson. He takes a risk every time he tries to steal second. Most of the time he makes it. Only you can know what risks are involved as you try to "steal second" in your career.

Study the following two exercises that involve risk-taking decisions. One is a business decision and the other a lifestyle decision. Think carefully about what expenditures might be called for in terms of time, money, energy, and popularity. Recall the examples of risk-takers that we've included in this chapter and use them for inspiration. These exercises are designed to test your willingness to take risks and point the way to developing persistence and confidence. Study them, and then if you're willing, answer the questions on a separate piece of paper.

Exercise No. 1

Assume you are the president of the Board of Education in a large city. You are responsible for school budgets, the curriculum being taught, the athletic program, extracurricular activities such as school bands and clubs, and negotiating contracts with teacher associations. The city in which you live has become quite concerned by a rapid increase in teenage pregnancies, resulting in school dropouts. You realize that the majority of students in middle school and high school do not understand the factors involved in birth control. You also understand the issue is an emotional one, involving family values.

Now, a course in sex education for students in the age group most concerned is offered. The cost in terms of money is simply the cost of the materials, books, and films. The cost in terms of parental concern about you and the school board's decision is hard to figure. You know that in other school districts that proposed a sex education program there was a roar of protest from parents and outrage on the part of community leaders. Yet the fact remains, this course could very well mean a decrease in teenage pregnancies. You are aware, although parents may not be, that this is not a course that encourages sex experimentation, abortion, or birth control measures. Rather, its emphasis is on abstinence and self-control.

1. Do you feel that education in school on the subject is better than leaving it up to parents or student peers?
    ___ Yes ___ No
2. Are you prepared to face a storm of protest from parents or other groups?
    ___ Yes ___ No
3. Are you willing to risk your popularity, even a possible call for your resignation?
    ___ Yes ___ No
4. Do you feel the subject is too important to be ignored in this day of greater freedom from parental restraints?
    ___ Yes ___ No

If you can honestly answer *yes* to the four questions, you can honestly feel you are a calculated risk-taker. You have, in this case, considered the results to be worth the personal cost.

If you answered *no*, write down your reasons for doing so and then analyze them. Consider why you felt you could not take the risk. It will provide insights for you in future risk-taking in your own personal situations.

Exercise No. 2

Assume you live in a normally quiet neighborhood, perhaps a tree-shaded suburb. You know some of your neighbors, but not all. In the house next to yours a new, middle-aged couple with no children recently moved in. You hardly know them, but you have spoken briefly when seeing them outdoors.

One night you are awakened about 2 a.m. by the sound of yelling and screaming next door. You have no way of knowing if the newly moved-in couple are fighting, or if one or the other is guilty of spouse abuse, or if one or the other has been hurt and is in extreme pain, or if the sounds you hear are actually coming from a late-night television program that has been turned on too loud. You get up, go to the front porch and glance over to the house next door. You see the lights are on. You also notice that other houses have their lights on as neighbors besides yourself have heard the yelling. However, no one has made an effort, as you have, to look out and see what might be the problem or if there's need for help.

1. In this situation, would you get dressed and go next door even though you might find yourself in the midst of a violent, domestic quarrel that can perhaps result in an injury?
___ Yes ___ No

2. Would you seek another neighbor's help and then go next door to see what's up?
___ Yes ___ No

3. Would you telephone next door to see if you can be of any help, risking a "none of your business," instead of a punch in the nose?
___ Yes ___ No

4. Would you call the police and have them drop by at your neighbor's, but ask them not to mention that it was you who called?
___ Yes ___ No

5. Do you feel that it's none of your business, and you should just forget it and go back to bed?
___ Yes ___ No

This is a moral as well as a physical personal dilemma. It can be one where a risk taken is a foolish one, or it can be one where the risk is calculated and possibly worthwhile. If you answered *yes* to questions 1 and 2, you are probably taking a foolish risk. If you answered *yes* to questions 3 and 4, you are probably taking a calculated risk. If you answered *yes* to question 5, you're taking no risk at all. Analyze your answers to see how willing you are to take risks in situations that have nothing to do with mastering your way to the top. Answers to such risk-taking questions can provide a clue as to how willing you are to take risks in business situations. You may have thought you were willing to tackle anything involving risk only to find out you may be lacking courage in one area or another. If that is so, you need to work extra hard at the *be a risk-taker* step, in order to master your way to the top.

6
Pump Up
Your Confidence

AT THE TIME I sold cars for a living, I'd size up a prospect and more often than not would sell a car with more standard features and options than had been asked for. Sometimes prospects aren't able to tell their wants from their needs. Needs can be fulfilled when someone stretches a confidence muscle to reach it.

When I put a prospect in a better car and made the sale, several pleasant results occurred. Of course, the car had increased value when it came to a trade-in. Also, the customer was more likely to look at the new car as an investment rather than as a purchase. But there was another, more subtle factor.

When I put the keys to the new car in the customer's hand, I'd say, "I congratulate you on your show of self-assurance, of self-confidence."

"What do you mean?" the customer would ask.

"Well, a new, higher-priced car doesn't say very much about the car except value and prestige. However, it says a lot about you. That new car shows how you feel about yourself. You took a giant step forward, and you wouldn't have done that if you didn't feel you could handle it."

Confidence is the muscle that lets you tackle risk-taking

and win. You don't need an instructor at a health and fitness spa to tell you that muscle doesn't just happen. Muscles need to be developed through exercise or working out. Body builders call that "pumping iron."

Your confidence muscle—your self-assurance—can be developed by what I call "pumping confidence," or simply beefing it up. It begins with *believing in yourself.*

I Believe in You

I tell my audiences that I believe in them. And I really do. When I look out at a sea of expectant faces, people who want to better their lives and are making the effort to do that, I can't help but be supportive. Then I always say, "What's more important is, do *you* believe in *you*?"

Do you remember the confident young man in the hit Broadway musical and movie *How to Succeed in Business Without Really Trying*? The show was based on the best-selling book of the same name, written by Shepherd Mead. I really enjoyed the book, but for me, I was trying to succeed in business by trying.

In the musical version, Robert Morse sang a song to himself, a song full of humor yet filled with self-belief. The song was called "I Believe in You." But the title of the show misleads. The young man did succeed, but only by trying. As I recall it, that young man took his first confident step from a window-washer's scaffold into a business office, a place completely foreign to him. And there, from the mailroom, he persevered until he was chairman of the board.

An even more confidence-promoting story lies behind the musical production. Abe Burrows, the co-author of the stage version, and Frank Loesser, the composer of the music, had a track record in the theater. They had scored a big hit with *Guys and Dolls*, based on Damon Runyon stories. It took a great deal of confidence, however, to turn *How to Succeed in Business*, a book that had little or no plot, into a musical. There were naysayers, of course, who insisted that Burrows, who also directed the show, couldn't make it work.

Burrows proceeded with his collaborators to beef up his confidence muscle. He turned a deaf ear to detractors. Did his confidence pay off? You bet. *How to Succeed* won the Pulitzer Prize.

That's not all. Consider the self-confidence shown by one of the show's major stars. He had been an orchestra leader and singer since his college days. When he played the saxophone it wouldn't quit. He was the first to be dubbed a crooner some time before Bing Crosby. He was known coast to coast as the "Vagabond Lover." He had a long and successful career in radio. He made many appearances in successful films, most of them hits at the box office. Were there any worlds waiting to be conquered? You bet.

He was approached with the idea of joining the cast of *How to Succeed*. When asked if he could switch to something 180 degrees different, he replied that he could. When asked what made him think so, he replied that he had the confidence to do so.

He was right. Rudy Vallee, at age sixty, became a bright star again on Broadway, bringing down the house every night. Not only that, he repeated his role six years later in the movie. At age sixty-six, his confidence muscle had never become flabby.

You have to believe in yourself, because if you don't, nobody else will. Strong self-confidence is needed in order to master your way to the top.

Remember the bedtime story by Watty Piper called "The Little Train That Could"? It had to get to the top of the hill. So as it puffed along it kept saying "I think I can, I think I can, I think I can." It was confidence and persistence that kept that train chugging along on its way to the top. That train really believed in itself.

The worlds of yesterday and today are full of people who overcame or are overcoming great obstacles that challenge confidence and belief in oneself. Many have been an inspiration to me in the past; many more are an inspiration to me now.

Stepping Out with Confidence

I always admired the actor Herbert Marshall for his performances in movies, particularly *Duel in the Sun*. I admired him even more because of something I learned about him. He lost a leg in wartime military action. Now, that's bound to be a painful, disheartening experience for one whose career depended on graceful movement and an easy-going charm. Marshall is an example of confidence. He was outfitted with a prosthesis and he practiced walking. With each movement his self-assurance, his belief in himself, grew. The day came when he stepped out before an audience in a theater and before the cameras in a movie studio. He knew, he firmly believed, that he could carry it off. And carry it off, he did. To this day, thousands of his admirers do not know that Herbert Marshall had an artificial leg. His self-confidence shines through as brightly today on people's VCRs, as it did when he was at the peak of his career.

A Self-Confident Human Dynamo

Don Tocco, a personal friend, mastered his way to the top by building from scratch a national marketing company for a select group of contractors that construct manufacturing plants across the nation. Don Tocco is a strong believer in affirmation. He'll stand in a cold shower and say out loud, "I am a living, breathing, human dynamo!" Maybe he feels that will warm the water.

There were days when Don needed such affirmation to give himself a jump-start, not only in business but in life. He grew up in a low-income family. His childhood and teen years were spent in a difficult home environment marked by substance abuse and emotional abuse. Don channeled his energy from this negative atmosphere and adversity into sports—basketball, football, and baseball, in school as well as in city leagues. His grandparents were supportive, but he never had a mentor to counsel and guide him.

Tocco became a college dropout, with no business background. "I went to work for a cosmetics company," he said, "one of those multilevel franchise organizations. I invested borrowed money, and within a year I lost not just my shirt but everything."

After that venture, Tocco had ten different jobs before, out of sheer desperation, he got the idea of representing contractors, which was a sharp turn from anything he had done before. He was in debt to the tune of $7,500; all he had going for him was a never-wavering enthusiasm.

It's been said by many naysayers that enthusiasm is no substitute for experience. "Don't you believe it," Tocco states. "Enthusiasm is an attitude, and it can be as important to one's success as academic achievement or technical expertise," as he explains in his booklet "Your Success Formula." From a man in debt, Don Tocco managed to get one important contractor to agree to let him represent him. For three years he barely managed to make ends meet. His game plan was survival.

Survive, he did. Today, D. L. Tocco and Associates, Inc., as the marketing arm of a growing number of contractors, does over $100 million a year in sales. And the aggregate sales for those contractors will be over $2 billion dollars.

Such success didn't just happen. Don Tocco devised a roadmap for mastering his way to the top. Here are some of his benchmarks along the way:

1. Whatever your product or service, recognize your business as a "people business." Never fail to show people respect and courtesy.
2. Learn from your customers what they expect and demand. Then instead of giving them 100 percent, give them 110 percent.
3. Build loyalty. Win the confidence of your customers so that they will buy in all economic cycles because of your mutual allegiance. *Care* about your customers.
4. Never lose your self-confidence. Confidence is the self-assurance that if you provide good service, you'll *know* that things will turn out all right.
5. Watch *who* you are. Always remember "your character is showing." General Norman Schwarzkopf told me that "Leadership is a potent combination of strategy and character. But if you must be without one, be without the strategy."

To make sure he wouldn't lose his way, Tocco decided at an early age to abide by certain self-disciplines. "I determined to be careful about the data I allow to enter my mind. For twenty-five years I haven't allowed electronic junk—sleaze TV programs, trash newspaper articles, and sob stories about people. Who needs it? I watch little TV and read few magazines."

Tocco is a friend of actor Hugh O'Brian whom you will remember for his TV role as Wyatt Earp. O'Brian is deeply involved in working with young people, conducting leadership seminars in thirty countries. The program also reaches students at 13,000 high schools through regional programs. Tocco speaks annually at the Hugh O'Brian Youth (HOBY) International Leadership Seminar, and also at high schools and colleges throughout the United States and Mexico. "I believe that if you give people the building blocks of inspiration and hope," he says, "they'll internalize them and their souls will be open to achievement."

I've adapted a simple exercise from Don Tocco's "Your Success Formula," a booklet he hands out to people young and old alike. Consider each of these questions carefully and answer them as honestly as you can.

On a sheet of paper, write down these questions and your answers.

1. What do I enjoy doing most?
2. What are the things I do well?
3. What don't I enjoy?
4. What do I put my faith in?
5. How often do I say "I can't"?
6. What achievement is a burning desire with me?
7. How much do I like myself?

Study your answers carefully. Taken collectively, they form a profile, perhaps to your surprise, of your current self-confidence. For example,

- Your answers to questions 2, 4, and 7 point to what you may need to do or not do concerning your self-confidence.
- Your answers to questions 1, 2, and 6 may help you set goals.
- Your answers to questions 3 and 5 may help you detect negative thoughts about yourself and others.

Don Tocco is an inspiration to me and to untold others. His enthusiasm, his self-confidence, is contagious. From the most humble of beginnings to an office high up in a southern

Michigan skyscraper, this "human dynamo" is literal proof that he has mastered his way to the top.

If he can do it, so can you. (However, I'm not sure you have to stand under a cold shower to affirm your own dynamism.)

Self-Confidence Comes from Working Smart

I once had my self-confidence seriously wounded. I call the healing process another example of working smart.

There was a time in my automotive selling career when every month I would send out letters to customers as well as to prospects in my prospect file who hadn't bought after I had tried my level best to sell them. They were simple letters that asked customers and their families how they enjoyed the car. Were they satisfied? Could I be of further service? Or, I'd inform a prospect that some time had elapsed, and were they now ready to trade on a fine new car? My letters had two purposes: I wanted to make sure people remembered me and I wanted to keep my foot in the door. But I was amazed at what little response I got from those people—in fact, zip, zilch, goose egg. My self-confidence as a letter writer sank as low as a snake's belly.

Gaining or restoring confidence doesn't just happen. As I've said, you have to work at it—you have to exercise the confidence muscle. I finally figured out what was wrong. The time I mailed my letters—the beginning of the month—was a stupid choice. And the obvious dealership identification on the envelope was a mistake. So I started to work smart.

Each month when my letters went out to names on my mailing list, I sent them in different-size and color envelopes. I put regular postage stamps on them, not meter mail. For all a customer or prospect knew, it could be an invitation to a wedding or a card from dear Aunt Millie. Now, ten times out of ten my mail got opened and read, instead of being thrown in the wastebasket with dealership junk mail.

Also, I stopped sending them out at the first of the month, when bills usually flood a customer's mailbox. Most people—in fact, almost all people—do not regard bill time as a happy time.

I began to send my mail twelve times a year when people would not be in a bill-payment bad mood. Now my mail showed up in homes at a pleasanter moment.

The responses were now a turnabout. Many people acknowledged my mail with phone calls. They would say: "You are the only salesman that didn't forget me after you made the sale!" My sales increased, and so did my self-confidence about reaching people, pushing their hot buttons and getting them to welcome my "foot in the door."

Who Loves Ya, Baby?

Aside from your wife, sweetheart, or companion, it's probably your best friend who loves you. But here's a bit of Girard advice: *Be your own best friend.* If you are your best friend, it follows you're bound to like yourself. The more you like yourself, not out of conceit or on an ego trip, the more people will like you. Knowing that, your self-confidence grows. As you head for the top, you'll find there'll be days when you'll need a best friend— days that you'll need all the fire and drive that you can muster. Always remember that the fire and drive needed to get to the top is rooted in self-confidence.

Fire and Drive

Some years ago, during the winter, a man stopped at the dealership where I worked. Now, if you've never met a Michigan winter, you should know that a January day can be as cold and miserable as the heart of Scrooge in *A Christmas Carol.* On that particular day the weather was nearly a blizzard. The temperature was dropping by the hour, the snow piling deeper. The roads were like glass.

At that time I saw customers only by appointment. The man had no appointment. He didn't even have an overcoat. In no way was he dressed to cope with the weather. He had come to the dealership by bus. He was badly in need of a car. He had saved a hundred dollars for a down payment. That's all. He had been turned down by other dealerships because he could not get credit.

His name was Joe Scaglione. One glance at him and I knew he had hit rock bottom. I saw the hurt in his eyes. When I looked at him I saw myself as I once was. I knew what it was like to be down and out, yet determined not to be counted out. There was something in this man that convinced me he wanted another shot at life.

The priest at the monastery that I spoke of earlier once told me, "Joe, when you've been given a helping hand, a good way to repay it is to help another." I had been given more than one helping hand by that priest, so I determined to give this customer the shot of life that he needed.

I managed to get him credit (the details don't matter), and put him in the most basic wheels in the store. As I gave him the keys and after he expressed his thanks, I said; "Two things rest on this deal. My name and yours. Your good name starts with a good credit rating. Keep it that way. I've got confidence in you. More important, do you have confidence in yourself? Pump up your confidence every day of your life. Don't let me down."

He never did. Today, Joe Scaglione has a number of high-priced cars, foreign and domestic, in the wide driveway of his beautifully furnished home. He has wide acreage and a swimming pool the size of Rhode Island—all because of the fire and drive that stokes his confidence machine. From the day he walked in my dealership, his has been a success story, yet with struggles and setbacks, lows as well as highs.

As I've said, I keep in touch with customers. Some time after the winter storm, Scaglione told me, "Joe, you challenged me to be self-confident. I started to beef it up the day I drove off in the snow. All my life I've wanted to be the very best at whatever I did. You gave me the confidence to drive to the top."

I followed his career. He became a successful hairdresser, with his own salon for a dozen years. After those years of "hands on" hair care, he branched out into marketing hair-care products. Along the way he raised a family. He and his wife, Barbara, are the distributors throughout Michigan and four Canadian provinces for one of the most famous hair-care products in the world, Nexxus.

Was Joe Scaglione's rise in the business world the result solely of his pumping up confidence and receiving the help and support of his wife? Of course not. What else did he do along the way to the top? He worked smart, and the smarter he worked, the more his self-confidence grew.

Joe Scaglione went to school, determined to be the best hairdresser he could be. When he opened his own salon, he devoted hours to learning the "science" of hair. He attended seminar after seminar in the United States and abroad. He associated with top people in the business. He took risks along the way. When he sensed an opportunity, he grabbed it. All of that took self-confidence, fueled by his desire to be the very best at whatever he did.

I saw that in him when I sold him that car on that cruel winter day. All I did was to help kick his self-confidence into gear.

Eliminate the Negative

Remember, the best way to accentuate the positive is to eliminate the negative, as the song goes. When people with little confidence in themselves—the moaners and groaners, the "poor me's"—try to undermine your self-confidence, tell those chickens to "go scratch somewhere else." Broom them. I say "chickens" because those kind of people remind me of the story of Chicken Little.

Remember? She was scratching around by the henhouse, never looking up as she pecked. An acorn fell on her head. She ran around yelling to all who'd listen, "Dear me, the sky is falling, the sky is falling!" If other chickens had listened—those who looked at the dark side of everything—they would have lost all confidence not only in the sky but in themselves.

This is an example of negative thinking. But does that mean you can't go around without ever having a negative thought? Certainly not. People who go around with a perpetually beaming face and practice positive thinking every waking moment can become positive bores. No, you're not going to hinder your way to the top by a negative thought now and then. Every negative thought simply reaffirms a positive thought.

Dr. Paul Pearsall, the neuropsychologist and author of self-help best-sellers, believes that negative thinking fulfills one's life because then you can see both sides—there would never be ups without downs. But the point to remember is that you must not let a negative thought destroy your confidence. The sky is *not* falling.

Learn from Mistakes, Learn from Failure

A negative thought is just a thought. It doesn't do any harm unless it's put into action. A few months ago, a young real estate agent came up to me at the conclusion of a lecture. He said, "Mr. Girard . . ."

"Call me Joe." I always try to break down the walls of formality.

"All right," he continued. "I try to think positively and I

manage to do so most of the time. I can't understand why, in spite of positive thinking, I still make mistakes." He looked so concerned that I hastened to put him at ease.

"I just made one this morning," I said. "I forgot to change to a different flight, and I've missed mine, so I'll have to go standby and see what happens." That loosened him up a bit. "The point is, have I learned anything? Sure, I'll be more careful about watching my schedule in the future. No big deal, but a mistake is a mistake." Then, I gave him a challenge. I asked him to sit down and list three major mistakes that he felt he had made at his job or in his life.

He was back with his list in twenty minutes. As I remember it, what he wrote could be boiled down to this:

1. Dropping out of college in his final year.
2. Leaving his hometown and moving to the big city.
3. Dropping a bundle at the race track just a month earlier.

We sat down to talk them over, to see if we could pin down the *why* of what he considered mistakes.

He felt he didn't need a college education, so he quit campus life. Now he'd discovered that a degree would give him an edge. What could he do about it? Without any prompting from me he said he could go to night classes and in a short time earn the credits he needed. As though he had discovered the secret of perpetual motion, his face lit up and he vowed he'd finish his schooling.

He left his hometown because he felt the grass was greener elsewhere. It wasn't; he wasn't happy. He knew how to sell real estate. Again, with no prompting, he said, "I'll get that degree and then move back to where my roots are."

He liked horse racing. Nothing wrong with that—it's called the sport of kings—but he had played hunches, and hunches rarely win. I'm not a gambler, and he admitted he wasn't either.

He'd been foolish. Remember, "A fool and his money are soon parted." He said it himself. He also said that from then on he would allow himself only to bet so much money at the track—just what he could afford to lose. I believed him.

He said, "Thanks for helping me, Joe."

If he wanted to think I had, that was okay. Actually, he had helped himself. Just talking things over with someone gave him insights. I sent him on his way with, "Keep on thinking positive thoughts, and it's okay to fall on your face once in a while. Just learn something from it so you don't make the same mistake twice."

Mistakes made along the way to the top—those human errors that we fall prey to—have a way of shattering our self-confidence. That's less likely to happen if you tell yourself that it's okay to make mistakes. Everyone does. Psychologists like to call them "learning experiences." That's true if you *really* learn from them and move on. When you do, your self-confidence is restored.

A mistake doesn't necessarily mean failure; however, don't be afraid of failure. Most of us fail at something or other during our lives—exams in school or for a needed license; a tryout for a team or an audition for a part; a business venture or a deal gone sour. I've tasted failure in the home-building business. If I could bounce back, so can you.

The problem is that in our fear of failure, we try to avoid failure by never taking risks. The result is that we often miss out on many opportunities for success. A lost opportunity can be as confidence shattering as failure. At the same time, as you learned in Chapter 5, when you make a leap into the unknown you usually find yourself out of your "comfort zone."

Nobody could be more out of his comfort zone than a member of the armed forces who finds himself in a hostile situation. That's when the adrenaline takes over so that the soldier can cope with the situation. The French historian Alphonse de Lamartine put it this way: "Man . . . rushes into the thickest of the fight and amid the uproar of the battle regains confidence in himself."

When you find yourself out of your comfort zone, whether because of a major mistake or a failure or because of a situation not of your making, feel the adrenaline of your self-confidence pumping in. It will, if you reaffirm to yourself that *it's okay to make mistakes* and *it's no disgrace to have a failure*. Repeat that to yourself every morning. It will help you get rid of guilty feelings—guilty feelings are negative. Then study your mistakes and failures, if any, so that you learn from them and are less likely to repeat them.

Belief and Faith in Yourself

Baseball is America's national sport. Every pitcher puts his career on the line when he winds up for the throw. Every batter does the same thing, facing the call of a strike or making a swing at a fast ball or blasting the pitch right out of the park. Every batter has to step up to the plate with confidence if he wants to come through for his club.

I like to think that Hank Aaron started to pump up his confidence muscles as he moved from the on-deck circle to at-bat. I like to think his confidence muscle was as strong as his powerful shoulders and arms. He had to believe that when at the plate he'd get a hit or another run batted in.

His self-confidence, his belief in himself, paid off. He broke Babe Ruth's lifetime record of home runs and wound up his fantastic career with 735 of his own.

I recently received a letter from a forty-six-year-old Pennsylvania man in the insurance business. He stated that for fourteen years he had never been even remotely successful. After struggling most of the time he quit the business and worked at other jobs. He read what I had to say about confidence in *How to Sell Yourself*. "I now understand," he wrote, "that I really haven't had any self-confidence or faith in myself and in my ability." He stated that I have given him hope that he could do better, hope that he could build self-confidence, hope that he could develop a business that helps many people. He returned to the insurance business. I'm betting on him because *understanding* the need for self-confidence is the first step in pumping it up.

The things I've learned for myself and the things I've learned from others about building self-confidence can be summarized in these attitudes and actions:

1. Desire to be the very best at whatever you wish to do.
2. Put your fire and drive to work and work smart.
3. Say "I think I can, I think I can, I think I can." Nobody ever got anywhere except nowheresville by saying "I can't."
4. Dream the impossible dream, then wake up and go for it.
5. Be the master of your fate and the captain of your soul.
6. Have confidence in others so they'll have confidence in you.
7. Associate with confident people; broom away the moaners and groaners.
8. Know that it's okay to make mistakes, but learn from them.
9. Understand that it's no disgrace to fail. Start over.
10. Make belief in yourself a top priority.

The last item—belief in self—is the most important of all. Belief in one's self is the daily bench press that beefs up your ability to overcome obstacles, and puts muscle into your self-assurance. I believe in you as number one. Now believe in yourself!

7
How to Remember You're Number One

E VERY NOW AND then it's good to be reminded just who you are—especially if you're somebody.

Famous people don't need to be reminded, but the media, especially the supermarket scandal sheets, never let them forget that the public eye, particularly the camera, is always focused on them. Political figures, Hollywood and TV stars, sports personalities, and others in the news—protest as they might—are glad to receive their share of what publicity agents call "ink."

But you and I don't have a publicity agent. As a rule nobody is running around trying to plant a story about you in the press. Unless publicity is very important in your rise to the top, be glad that nobody's blowing your horn.

Who then will blow it? You, of course.

You have to blow your own horn, but in such a way that you don't turn off others by a *show of ego*. It's nice to know that others might think of you as number one. It's more important that you *know* you're number one.

At the beginning of this book you learned that it was important to see yourself as number one. You also learned that you needed to never let go of that picture of yourself. It's the picture of success; stick with it.

Remain Steadfast

One of my personal heroes was Winston Churchill, the British prime minister. Many historians consider him second in importance only to Benjamin Disraeli, who was prime minister during the nineteenth century when the sun never set on the British Empire. When it came to never letting go, of holding steadfast to your image as number one, Disraeli put it this way: "The secret of success is constancy of purpose." Constancy, or steadfastness, in mastering the steps on the way to the top is one way to remind yourself that you are number one. Say it to yourself every day.

You can say it to others, too, without making a big deal of it. One way is to wear a small "No. 1" pin in your lapel. They can be bought or you can have one made. You know by this time that I always wear one. At lectures to salespeople, individuals often come up to me, see the pin, and say, "So that's what reminds you that you are the world's number one salesman!"

My answer surprises them: "No, that pin reminds me that I'm number one in *all* things—at my work, at play, and with my family. It's a constant reminder." At that point I look down the length of the auditorium. I point out that when I look straight ahead I can see both side walls, the ceiling, and the floor without moving my eyes. Even so, my left eye will pick up the spark from the pin. I tell these individuals that even though I have my eyes on the big picture, that little pin sends me a signal as to where I fit in.

Whatever goal you're striving for, whatever top is there to be mastered, whatever your "big picture," have something to remind yourself that you're *somebody* in that big picture—that you're number one.

For example, I know a young man who owns a busy drive-through car wash and who has his eye on another. His goal is to build a chain of such car washes in his city, and he vows he will do it before, as he says, he winds up "in the big car wash in the sky." Meanwhile, he's looking out for number one. But does he wear a No. 1 pin as I once suggested? No. He wears a four-leaf clover pin in his lapel. People say to him, "That's a charm for good luck in your business, right?" He grins and replies, "Luck has nothing to do with it. I wear it to remind me that when—not if—I succeed in my goal, it will be because of my *own* efforts, and not because of lucky breaks or that old lady luck sure smiled at me."

So say or wear whatever works for you to help you remember that you're number one. Say it to yourself often or wear something on your person to remind you.

Don't Be a Blowhard

A great many people try to convince themselves that they are number one by telling others. Sometimes it works, often it doesn't.

There's not much on record to indicate that Muhammed Ali shouted "I am the greatest!" to himself, but he sure said it often enough to others. Whether it was to prove it to himself or simply to psych-out heavyweight challengers can be debated for hours. I know a great many people who feel that the more often Ali shouted his superiority, the less they thought of him— not as a champion boxer but as a person.

I've mentioned many times that you are what you believe. I'm pretty sure that Muhammed Ali believed what he said about himself. "I am the greatest" is certainly self-affirmation. The point is, whatever your affirmation, don't be obnoxious about it. If you want others to believe that you are number one, remember the familiar and very true saying: Actions speak louder than words. It's amazing how many loudmouths forget that.

Consider those people in the public eye who *showed* people that they're number one in their fields without having to *tell* people the fact every time they opened their mouths. If they ever thought they were number one, I'm willing to bet they affirmed it only to themselves.

Mahatma Gandhi—nonassuming, quiet, humble—was a man who never had to tell anyone *who* he was. Yet this number one leader steadfastly forged ahead to earn India its independence. Jerry Lewis, comic actor, keeps quiet about himself, but every year he *shows* he's a number one person with his nonstop telethon on behalf of kids stricken with muscular dystrophy.

Alfred Sloan, president and former board chairman of General Motors, the company which made the cars I sold, proved that he was number one by his position in the automotive industry. He was a man known for his great charities, and the Sloan-Kettering Institute for Cancer Research in New York is silent testimony of this and of his concern for others.

The detailed pictures of the American Southwest by noted photographer Ansel Adams speak for themselves, without Adams having told you that he was number one in his field.

Danny Kaye entertained millions with his flair for acting and singing. He could make you laugh with his comic abilities. Yet he was modest about his talent; he was even more modest about something else. His quiet efforts on behalf of UNICEF, the United Nations International Children's Emergency Fund, revealed this number one person's deep concern for disadvantaged children worldwide.

The former governor of my state and one-time mayor of Detroit, Frank Murphy, was basically a shy and retiring man. He mastered his way to the top by reaffirming his belief in himself—one that told him he could be anything he wanted to be. The steps along the way: mayor of Motown; governor-general and U.S. high commissioner of the Philippines; U.S. attorney general; and, ultimately, an associate justice of the U.S. Supreme Court. He never needed to tell a soul that he was number one.

But for visual evidence, there is the Frank Murphy Hall of Justice in my city—a number one symbol too big to wear on one's lapel.

The world is full of people who are number one, and who let you know it through their deeds and attitudes, even if they don't wear a lapel pin. This is true of the past and it's true today. I'm sure you can come up with a lengthy list of famous people who quietly went on being number one. You probably have friends and relatives who fit the description.

By the same token, the world is full of people who feel they have to shout it from the rooftops—to convince themselves and others how important they are, how they know they're number one. Shouting it is one thing; keeping it in proper perspective is another. That's the hard part.

Just Who Do You Think You Are?

Frequently when I lecture I ask some members from the audience to come up onto the platform—maybe a half dozen people—and ask them to tell me they're number one.

I ask them to shout out loud and clear to the audience, "I AM NUMBER ONE!" It's fun to hear them yell their lungs out. Then the hard part begins. I ask one, "Just what does being number one mean to you?"

"It means I'm the *first*," is the usual response.

I ask the others on the platform the same question. I get the same response. "I'm the first!"

I look at them and then wink at the audience. "Well, if you're first," I say to the first person I asked the question, "and the others say the same thing, where does that leave you? You can't all be first, can you?" The point is that when you see yourself as number one, you need to do so in relationship to others who affirm that they're also number one.

I tell them the story of John Hancock. This great figure of our American revolution was the first to step up to sign the

Declaration of Independence. He wrote his signature in very large letters—so big you'd think he was trying to hog the page. Because the signature stood out so much, we use the expression even today for signing something: "Put your John Hancock on it." After Hancock signed the Declaration, the other fifty-five signers from the thirteen colonies had to squeeze in their names. Although Hancock's signature was larger than the others, their names on the document were just as important as his. He was *number one, but he was only first among equals.*

Everyone on the platform with me, I point out, is first among equals. The ancient Greek, Aesop, said in one of his fables, "Be content with your lot; one cannot be first with everything." I say hogwash! You can be first, you can be number one. Just remember that you are first among equals.

The foreman of a jury is no more than first among equals. The Roman Catholic pope, the Bishop of Rome, is first among all other bishops. The playing captain of a hockey or other sports team is simply the first among other teammates who are equally important.

The John Hancock story always helps me make that important point. I like history. I've had little classroom experience, but as Mark Twain said, "I've never let schooling get in the way of education." Who am I to quarrel with that Mississippi riverboat pilot and great American author? If he could be self-educated, I once told myself, so can I. I say the same to you about mastering your way to the top: if I can do it, so can you.

Varley O'Connor, the author of *Like China*, writes about a character who has a small plaque on her desk that reads: "Act as if, and you will be." Good advice. Act as if you're number one, and you will be. Soon you will get affirmation that you are number one.

Remembering that you are is an important signpost as you master your way to the top. Will Rogers, the great cowboy humorist, Ziegfeld Follies star, and movie actor, once said, "I never met a man I didn't like." He's been quoted repeatedly.

But *really* liking others begins with liking yourself. You can't be number one if you don't like yourself. I have a sign in my office. It's the first thing people see when they enter. It says "I like you!" But I could never have said that, and meant that, if first I didn't like who and what I was. I suspect Rogers felt the same way.

So reaffirm to yourself every day that you're number one. Act like it. Walk like a number one person, with your head held high and your shoulders back. Dress like a number one person in clothes appropriate to the situation. Talk like a number one person, watching your language, never gossiping. Like yourself as a number one person and then you'll like and treat others the same. And work smart like a number one person all the time.

Mr. Enthusiasm

Almost daily, listeners hear the voice of Ralph Nichols on radio commercials throughout Michigan. He urges people to grasp the opportunity to forge ahead in their careers—as he did. He is CEO of the Ralph Nichols Corporation. Since 1968, he has owned and operated under a license to promote Dale Carnegie courses. The courses are considered as licensees or sponsors, rather than as franchises, for Dale Carnegie. His outreach is all over Michigan and now extends into Ontario.

I suspect that practically everyone in the business world is familiar with Dale Carnegie's book, *How to Win Friends and Influence People*. This pioneer work in the field of self-help is the cornerstone of the Dale Carnegie courses.

I first met Ralph Nichols when he walked into my dealership office a few years ago. He said he wanted to shake my hand. Why? "You, Joe Girard, are what we teach," he said. "You are number one." He didn't have to tell me that he was number one in his field and in his life. His high-octane enthusiasm burst from every word he uttered. We have been friends ever since. He once gave me a variation on "the elevator is out of order" slogan. Ralph put it this way: "Step up the stairs or stare at the steps."

Nichols's father hailed from South Africa. He instilled in his son a love of reading and of strengthening his vocabulary. His background was a combination of chess and books, along with cricket and soccer. Above all, he developed a strong sense of self-discipline. He was on fire with the desire to succeed in life in order to justify his father's faith in him. With Nichols, this drive became what he calls a magnificent obsession—an obsession to be number one in whatever field he chose.

During a hitch in the U.S. Coast Guard he just happened to take a Dale Carnegie course. He was hooked. From then on, that concept was the compass that guided him into his career. Between the rugged training and discipline of the Coast Guard and the world Dale Carnegie opened up to him, Nichols firmly believed he could do anything he had to. If someone ordered him to stand on his head for a year, he knew he could do it. He could accomplish whatever task as long as he believed he could. He wound up teaching the Dale Carnegie course.

Nichols also gained something—a mentor. "The man was like a brother to me," Nichols says, "he was a friend, a buddy, a boss." That mentor, Bud Hogberg, instilled in him a number of important principles: study hard, get up in the middle of the night if you have to and make notes; always go the extra mile; believe in people and their worth; always risk on the side of optimism; do the things successful people do and that failures don't like to do; allow yourself to be embarrassed now and then; never be dissuaded from your goals; remember you are responsible for your own life; and save for the day you reach the top.

Nichols had a burning desire to be rich, not at the expense of someone else but just to be able to enjoy the good things in life. Remember when I covered the different ways people view success and I pointed out that there was nothing wrong with having money? Believing he was number one in all things, Nichols determined to pay himself first—that is, out of every hundred dollars he earned, he would pay himself ten, and bank it. Out of every thousand bucks, he'd bank a hundred, for that was how savings grew. Saving means that you don't spend what's banked, his mentor told him.

Nichols kept a crumpled note in his wallet. On it was written, "Do you need this?" Whenever he was tempted to spend money on something, he'd take out that note, which told him to think twice. It worked. From teaching the Dale Carnegie course to selling the value of it to others and signing up people to take the course, he finally saved enough to buy his own building and head his own corporation. He followed the principles he had learned, and he shares them enthusiastically with others. I call him Mr. Enthusiasm. He has never wavered, especially in his determination to master his way to the top.

Nichols doesn't brag about his achievements, so I'll brag for him. He's the number one Dale Carnegie promoter in the world, all because he reaffirmed to himself that he was number one. Most people hope for miracles. Number one people like Ralph Nichols *expect* them.

Remember that as number one you're the cream of the crop, and the cream always rises to the top.

8
Beware the Green-Eyed Monster

As you master your way to the top there are two words that you need to eliminate from your vocabulary: *jealousy* and *envy*. You know what they stand for, and you'll want to make sure that you don't let either of the two influence your attitudes and actions. It's not easy to do, but is absolutely necessary.

Jealousy is often called the green-eyed monster. Envy is listed as one of the seven deadly sins. You may not consider it a sin according to your religious beliefs, but envy can still be deadly.

If you harbor feelings of jealousy toward and envy of another, rest assured that it not only can hurt the person at whom those emotions are directed but can hurt you far more. Jealousy and envy are like a sickness, gnawing away at your insides. Also, your envy and jealousy of another's success may spur that person on to greater heights—something you hadn't bargained for at all. For example, jealousy by other salespeople simply was a challenge for me to set a new record for selling automobiles. Jealousy and envy rear their heads in every business.

Pause and Reflect

Take a moment to think about the tragic events in the world that are caused by jealousy and envy. In fact, it's pretty hard

85

to escape seeing the results of those two emotions. To many a family member they are close to home.

How much unhappiness is felt because someone eats his or her heart out because of what someone else has in their business and/or personal life? How much spouse abuse is the result of jealousy? And where there is spouse abuse, child abuse is often not far behind.

How many marriages are wrecked by jealousy? Sometimes the jealousy is real, sometimes it's imagined. How many suicides have resulted from jealousy or envy or both? How many people have spent time in jail because of someone's envy or jealousy? Jealousy by someone you don't even know can inconvenience you and cost you money, or even hurt you and your reputation.

Recently I received a telephone call from a gentleman in the Criminal Investigation Division (CID) of the Internal Revenue Service (IRS). Now that could make anyone's blood pressure go through the ceiling. The phone call was to acknowledge a letter written by *me*, a request that they look at my tax returns from 1984 onward and check into the fact that I had cheated on my expense accounts.

What? The fact is, of course, that I had never written such a letter. It had been mailed from Jacksonville, Florida, and it supposedly had my signature. I have been audited several times in the past ten years with no evidence of wrong-doing discovered.

The CID of the IRS was amazed by the letter. They said they had never before had anyone put the finger on himself. I told them how to tell the letter was phony: It had been signed *Girard*, whereas on tax returns I use *Girardi*. Also it did not include my social security number.

Of course, it cost me money to clear myself of something I had never done. My attorney requested all copies of correspondence concerning my personal income tax under the Freedom of Information Act. It was pointed out that I have made many enemies, owing to my years of successful competition in car sales. It was also pointed out that threats by phony letters were commonplace to me, and, more important, my life has been threatened on various occasions. I have been issued a gun permit. I am fed up with the many hoaxes directed my way, yet I realize that I will probably continue to be a victim of someone's jealousy because my name and business address are well known.

This personal situation regarding jealousy of my achievements, or the desire to get revenge for a business grudge, illustrates what it's like to be on the receiving end of envy. Can you imagine how you would feel if you let jealousy of another lead to an act causing pain or inconvenience or expense to the other person? Revenge is not sweet. Most often it backfires on the avenger.

Jealousy and envy are a sickness. Both are contagious. Usually the person who is jealous of another has a body and a mind full of poison. If you want to master your way to the top, and I know you do, then use police action to rid yourself of those self-destroying emotions.

I've seen many times the way envy and jealousy have destroyed a career. I've seen salespeople in the automotive field compete to be top salesperson of the month in retail sales or fleet sales. Unfortunately I've also seen fellow salespeople fail to step up their efforts to move cars from the showroom and onto the road. Instead of devoting time to prospecting, making cold calls, and following through on customers, they spend time and effort at the water cooler, knocking the other fellow who is working his butt off. They don't realize that every jealous knock is a boost for the hard-working guy.

I've had the heartbreak of seeing jealousy nearly destroy my family. Because someone envied my place in the *Guinness Book of Records*, he spread rumors that I had died. Before I learned of it, others had phoned my home, offering sympathy and asking what happened. Can you imagine what that jealous "hoax" did to my family? It's not hard to laugh off, even if Mark Twain did when he said, "The reports of my death are greatly exaggerated."

Be Proud, Not Jealous

When someone has achieved something of worth—a job promotion, a new car, a new home, a chance to travel—we often say, "Boy, do I envy you!" We may actually envy that person or we may not, but we use the expression to indicate admiration. It's a simple word, *envy*, but it's dangerous to use it. Every time we do, we plant it deeper into our psyches. Using the word simply underscores the feelings we have inside—the ones we don't express but which often control our actions.

To say you envy someone or are jealous of a person may be said lightly, and you may be convinced that you really don't harbor ill feelings. Still, it's better not to put the words into the air. We often live to regret using words that express hatred, loathing, suspicion, contempt. I put words that indicate jealousy and envy in the same category, especially the words themselves.

Remember the saying you used as a kid—"Sticks and stones may break my bones but names can never hurt me"? It's not true. Names can hurt people. Don't say anything that might indicate you are jealous of another. You can keep from *saying* it if you make sure you aren't *feeling* it.

Detroit is often called Motown, just as New York is the Big Apple and Dallas is the Big D. One of the most successful recording industries in the country began in Detroit—Motown Records. From Motown came such headliners as the Supremes, Diana Ross, the Jackson Five, Smokey Robinson, Stevie Wonder, and Marvin Gaye. It's reasonable to assume that all of those performers might be the target of jealousy and envy on the part of other entertainers. In fact, probably no other people face as much jealousy as do actors, singers, and dancers by their fellow performers. Perhaps this is so because of the top incomes they earn, their popularity with fans, and the general clout they possess.

Every now and then entertainers still popular after twenty or thirty years will indicate support of new singers and dancers and actors. The best of a past generation have made it big, and they know envy and jealousy of newcomers are wasted emotions. The newcomers have to pay their dues just as the established ones did. Talent is what counts, wherever found, and the only emotion shown at another's achievements should be pride.

As you master your way to the top, turn envy and jealousy of others into pride in their accomplishments. Instead of saying, "I wish I were more like him or her," *do* something to be more like him or her. Why sit on the sidelines envying and being jealous of someone else when those feelings will never get you out of the dugout and up to bat?

You'll find mastering your way to the top tough going if you are worried about *what* others are doing and *how* they're doing. When you see someone who's doing well—succeeding, enjoying what he or she has earned—look to see what you can borrow from that person. Maybe it's a smile. Maybe it's an attitude, a good word, a fashion statement. Before you know it, you've kicked your jealousy out the window, and you've got your own stuff together.

Envy and jealousy are too big a load to carry on your back as you take the steps, one at a time, to the top.

Cause and Effect

Scientists and physicists know that for every cause there is an effect of one kind or another. In fact, the effect may also be a cause in itself, creating another effect. Cause, effect; cause, effect; cause, effect. Pressure builds up inside the earth (cause) and a volcano erupts (effect), with volcanic lava and ash pouring forth from the eruption (cause) so that mountainside villages are wiped out (effect). Such losses (cause) spur villages to rebuild their homes and their lives (effect). And so it goes.

The cause and effect of less earth-shattering events can be just as significant. When jealousy and envy are the cause, consider these resulting effects:

- *Murder.* Cain slew Abel because he was jealous of his brother.
- *Betrayal.* His brothers sold Joseph into slavery in Egypt because they were jealous that he was their father's favorite. They couldn't stand the sight of the coat of many colors that he wore.
- *Broken friendships.* I know of a middle-aged newspaper man who is jealous of his friend, a successful novelist. He envies the books his friend had published. At the same time, his novelist friend envies the newspaper man's nomination for a Pulitzer Prize for outstanding reporting on a nationwide story, a prize that the novelist is not even within shouting distance of receiving. The two friends no longer speak to each other.

The Girard Solution

Here's how to tame the green-eyed monster if you want to master your way to the top:

1. Think positive thoughts about other people, especially those whose success is likely to invite envy. Like those people for what they are and— this is important—for what they are not. That way you'll have little room in your mind for jealousy.
2. Vaccinate yourself against the infectious words,

envy and *jealousy*. Think of that scar on your
arm or leg as providing immunity from being jealous
of others or being a victim of envy.

3. To get rid of a bad habit, you substitute a good
   habit. Do the same with the green-eyed monster.
   Replace the monster words with others. For
   example, in your thinking, replace *jealousy* with
   admiration, and *envy* with *pride* when you view
   the accomplishments and successes of others.

4. Meditate often about what you should be doing and
   not what others have done. If others are worthy,
   meditate on how you can be more like them, rather
   than resenting what they've accomplished.

9
Four Strategies for Success

Strategy No. 1: Remember the Name!

This is the story of a man who rose from a small-town background to head one of the finest restaurant organizations in the Midwest. The late Winston "Win" Schuler took over his father's hotel dining room in the mid-1930s and turned that twenty-seat restaurant into a family business that later stretched the width of Michigan, a dining belt that buckled up the lower peninsula. *Travel-Holiday* magazine has listed the flagship restaurant as one of the country's finest eating places.

What's in a name? A lot. Especially if you catch a person's name, memorize it, and put it to good use. That was the strategy Win Schuler developed—one of many important methods he used to master his way to the top. Schuler had many techniques for memorizing, some tried-and-true and similar to those I mention in *How to Sell Yourself*, and some he created for his particular situation.

During the late 1920s, Schuler waited tables to put himself through college. After college he took a job as a teacher of American history, doubling also as football coach, at a high school on the isolated shores of Lake Superior. He was, before he took over his father's hotel restaurant in Marshall, Michigan, an active jock—a quarterback and halfback, a first baseman, and a guard in basketball. He made it a point to know his teammates' names as well as the names of those of the opposing teams. In 1940, he converted a building next to his father's hotel into a bowling alley.

In World War II, Schuler became a navy supply officer. While on a tour of duty in Washington, D.C., he had a chance to indulge his tastes in food—if not gourmet at least substantial—in some of the best mess halls in the capital: the cafeterias of the FBI, the Supreme Court, the Pentagon, and other government agencies. He managed to learn and remember the names of most fellow officers with whom he came in contact.

After the war, Win returned to Marshall and expanded the restaurant. A pin-boy strike caused him to close the bowling alley, and he remodeled it to become part of the restaurant. The place for strikes and spares became the Centennial Room, and the restaurant became headquarters for a series of dining establishments featuring hearty country cooking and friendly service. Win Schuler was on his way to becoming a self-made multimillionaire. Like myself, Schuler received the Golden Plate Award, given annually to the "movers and shakers of America" by the American Academy of Achievement.

Today, the company is headed by Win's son, Hans, and it includes his grandson, Larry—four generations of restaurateurs dedicated to serving the public. The Schuler restaurants are known state-wide. Schuler's is also famous for a zesty snack product that the young owner whipped up using the agitator of his washing machine: Bar-Scheeze. Was the spreadable cheese the secret of Schuler's success? In part, yes. But the main ingredient was that Schuler never forgot a person's name. He always welcomed customers as he would guests in his home. He remembered the name of every person with whom he made contact.

Of course, though Schuler's record in remembering names was impressive, it wasn't 100 percent—just 99 percent.

How did he do it? Every new person Schuler met, every customer, business associate, or employee, would be asked his or her name. The full name. Then Win Schuler would repeat the name *three* times. He'd find a way to do this naturally in any conversation that followed. After that, Schuler claims, he would remember the name forever.

Learn the name and never forget it. That was his philosophy. Of course, he had "tricks" to help him out. He'd eavesdrop at a restaurant table and pick up a name here and there. If there were four people to a table, he'd drop by, introduce himself, and get the names of the four patrons in return. Then he'd link them to north, south, east, and west: Smith, north; Jones, east; etc. If it was a round table seating six or eight people, he'd link them to the dial of his watch: Smith at two o'clock, Jones at eight, and so on.

He always wrote the names down. At night, before he went to sleep, he'd go over the names. Schuler felt that repetition was the cement of memory. Schuler's way is effective. Try it. It works.

Strategy No. 2: Stay on Course!

Jim Lipari is a man whose wholesale business grew from extremely humble beginnings. Indeed, the Lower East Side of Detroit is a place where, rounding a corner, you're apt to find yourself in the middle of a ghetto, in front of a thriving parish church, or in an area teeming with produce, meat, and fish markets. I suppose it's no different from the "lower east sides" of most big cities that were home to large numbers of immigrants—New York, Chicago, Seattle, San Francisco.

Detroit's Lower East Side was the birthplace of what was to

become Lipari Foods, a $35 million distributorship with fantastic warehouse space for frozen or refrigerated meat products, cheeses, baked goods, and other items that are then shipped to retail outlets in huge semi rigs throughout Michigan and Ohio.

Just out of the army, Jim Lipari went into business with his dad, who had a small mom-and-pop store. Jim hungered to be on his own. When the economy went bad, he had his chance. He hungered for success.

Lipari began to mix up a barbecue sauce that was given (or sold, when lucky) to relatives and friends. People liked its taste. They asked for it. Soon there was real demand. (The secret formula has long since been replaced, but Lipari still has in his office the very last bottle of the original barbecue sauce—a collector's item.) Jim Lipari then bought a small warehouse, cleaned it, painted it, and opened for business. He experimented with a spaghetti sauce. ("Who's Paul Newman?" he asks, grinning.)

But he knew that he had to sell more than just spaghetti, barbecue, and sloppy joe sauces. He went on the road in a station wagon, calling on retail outlets. Lipari was acting as manufacturer, broker, trucker, salesperson, and shelf-space servicer in the retail outlet. He wasn't succeeding.

You're probably several jumps ahead of me. Lipari was wearing too many hats. He was thinking like "big business," yet operating as a "small power." He was going off in all directions. One day I said to him, "Jim, you're like a ship without a rudder. You're zigzagging all over the place."

"What are you trying to tell me, Joe?" he asked.

"Stay on course. Decide what you really want to do most, then don't waver. Chart your course and stay on it."

That's exactly what he did, and Lipari credits "staying on course" as the most important technique he followed as he mastered his way to the top. First, he made a decision to get out of manufacturing products. Next, he decided to keep distributing food products, but no longer sauces. Then, he became a distributor of other manufacturers' products, putting a markup on them before selling them to retail outlets. Some would go out under their brand names; others would carry the Lipari Foods label.

He never veered off course. Naturally there were ups and downs along the way, but Lipari used his staying power to back up his planning and selling strategy. I know Jim well. I've watched his career. There hasn't been a zig or a zag in it since the day I told him to stop going whichever way the wind blew.

Today, his salespeople head out through Michigan and Ohio calling on supermarkets and independent retailers, and stocking their shelves and refrigerator and freezer sections with a wide variety of cheeses, salami, cold cuts, chicken, baked goods, sauces, vinegars, and other items. As Lipari watches his fleet of trucks move out, he looks back on the days when he, as a kid in hard times, decided to mix up barbecue and spaghetti sauces and sell them to make a buck. After realizing he was spreading himself too thin, he made "stay on course" his watchword, and he moved ahead.

Strategy No. 3: Pick from Your Menu!

I once met a man while flying to Las Vegas. He told me his strategy for success, then asked me not to use his name. After I agreed, he said that he recognized me from my picture on a book jacket, and that he was a wealthy rancher in New Mexico. I asked him if that was his "top" in life and in business.

"Of course. What else?"

"Forgive me," I said, "but doesn't being a successful rancher mean simply that you have lots of real estate, cattle or other live stock, lots of water, and a sure market for whatever you raise?"

He laughed. "Sure that's a requirement. I didn't get the

land by buying it. My daddy left it to me—land, buildings, everything. It was in pretty bad shape. Daddy was a dreamer. He never knew how to get a handle on what he had." He paused a moment and I could see he was deep in thought. "Mr. Girard . . ."

"Call me Joe."

"Okay. It's what you do with what you've got, the decisions you make, the goals you set out to reach. I inherited Daddy's land just in time. Another five years and he would have lost it all."

We were over the Mississippi River as he talked. "My daddy boasted about how much land he had and how long it would take to cross it on the back of one of his palominos. I visioned what the land could yield, how it could become productive and never in danger of being taken from me.

"I've read your books, Joe, never heard you lecture, and I like your ideas. But I don't sell things like you did. I didn't need info on how to make a presentation or how to close a sale. What I did was make up a menu and serve myself à la carte, as the high-class restaurants say."

"Menu?" I was puzzled.

"Sure. Just like you can't eat everything that pops up on a restaurant menu—you pick what appeals to you—I just can't do everything you advise at one sitting. Nothing says you have to take your ideas in order. One doesn't follow on the heels of the other, right?"

"Sure, just one step at a time."

"You got it. I took down your ideas on setting goals and keeping promises, on staying enthusiastic and remaining self-confident. I even made a bet with myself that I'd tell the truth—not even little white lies—for ninety days. That sure opened a lot of folks' eyes, including mine."

He explained that he took my ideas, and the effective techniques of others, and had his wife put them all together and enter them in her personal computer just as she did her recipes.

"Now, I have a menu full of ideas. Whenever I feel the need to satisfy my appetite—or help in making a decision or the courage to take a risk—I simply retrieve the technique on the PC. I pick and choose à la carte to meet a hunger need at the moment."

While he was talking I was reminded of a line from the movie *Auntie Mame*. In effect, life is a banquet, but most people never draw up a chair to the table to enjoy what life offers. I was intrigued by the rancher's idea of my techniques as "food for thought," with helpings to be taken when needed most— that everything could not be digested all at once.

Strategy No. 4: Seize the Day!

Many people miss an important step on their way to the top because they fail to recognize opportunity—even when it stares them in the face.

As the commercial for MasterCard puts it, you should master the opportunities. Remember the story of Joe Scaglione in Chapter 6? When he sensed he was in the presence of opportunity, he grabbed it. That's solid advice because, as the saying goes, opportunity seldom knocks twice.

A young produce manager in a supermarket once asked me, "Joe, how do you *know* when you're face-to-face with opportunity? How can you be sure?" It was a good question. I told him that it wasn't easy. The best answer, and I believe it to be good advice, is to trust your instincts. Go with your gut feeling. I wouldn't give such advice unless I knew it was sound. It's worked for me. On more than one occasion on the way to the top, I took a step simply because I had a strong gut feeling that it was the thing to do. Can this result in a misstep? Of course. When that happens, pick yourself up and start over again. Most of the time your gut feelings will be right.

Successful entrepreneurs are those who seize the day, who grab opportunity when it knocks. There was a copywriter who, some years ago, felt secure in his job at an advertising agency. He was good at his work and he knew it. He was highly regarded by his peers. Then one day he had the chance to go into partnership with another copywriter and form an agency of their own. Should he run the risk? Should he go for it or should he stay where he was? He decided to take the plunge. The waters were deep at first, and the partners treaded water for quite some time, but the young man has never regretted the move. The ad agency is prospering.

I know another gentleman who struck out from his well-paying, secure job to make a long-standing dream come true. He founded a school of small business management. He designed the courses, mapped out the school facilities, and later saw his efforts expand to various college campuses. He didn't wait—he seized the day.

And I know a technical writer of sales and service training materials who had spent his time writing for others. He decided that it was time to write for himself, and he formed his own communications company, working directly for businesses and industrial companies. Where other communication companies had put a "markup" on him when they sold his services, he now put that markup on his own services. He had to bite the bullet for a while, but his decision started to pay off and it's still doing so. He seized the day.

10
How to Stand on Your Own Two Feet

Iₙ ₜₒ—

I N TODAY'S BUSINESS world it's easier to be a conformist, to go along with the crowd, than it is to march to your own drum beat. To do so calls for self-reliance, the ability to stand on your own two feet, no matter what the crowd is doing, no matter what the thing of the moment happens to be.

Ralph Waldo Emerson said in his essay on self-reliance that "whoso would be a man must be a nonconformist." (Today, with the growing feminist influence in the business world, in the marketplace, in politics, and in law, Emerson's words apply equally to women.) When you've mastered your way to the top, you stand at the head of an "institution"—that is, it may be a department, a factory, a corporation, or an agency. Emerson also pointed out a truth that every business person needs to recognize: "An institution is the lengthened shadow of one man."

Who Calls the Shots?

Of course, the people I tell you about often needed and welcomed help from others. Mastering your way to the top never calls for refusing a helping hand. But remember that in the long run, you—like the people in the stories I relate—are the captain of your ship. You're controlling the rudder, and the ship will go where you steer it. This means:

- You must be the one to call the shots. After all, you might not like the aim of others.
- You must not dance to someone else's tune. Again, you may not like the music. Remember the old saying, "He who pays the piper calls the tune."
- You must rely on your own instincts as to what is right and what is wrong. The crews on Columbus's ships urged him to turn back, but he kept his course.
- You must learn to develop self-reliance. This is akin to self-confidence, but not quite the same. It's also akin to enthusiasm, which is the staying factor in self-reliance.

As you master your way to the top there'll be many moments when you look around and realize you're all alone. As they say, "It's lonely at the top." You'll suddenly think, "Who do I lean on? Who do I walk with? Who's guiding me over the rough spots?"

You know the answer: *you*. There you are, standing on your own two, stumbling feet. What you've got going for you is self-reliance. So kick out conformity! Refuse to be like "everyone else." Always try to do things that are right, that you know deep in your heart are *right* for you.

Even if you find yourself alone and different from other people, do what you think is right. Others may want you to conform, but it would be a dull world if everyone was the same. After all, no two fingerprints are the same, no two voiceprints are the same, not even two snowflakes are the same.

The rule to follow is this: When you stand on your own two feet in business and in life, make sure you let others enjoy the same privilege. Let them keep their footing. Let them help you, if need be, to keep yours.

Remember the fairy tale in which was asked, "Mirror, mirror, on the wall, who's the fairest of them all?" Make sure your image is an honest one of yourself. No matter who you listen to, your final stance has got to reflect your own thinking; you can't depend on someone else to do your thinking. President Harry Truman summed it up with the plaque that rested on his desk in the oval office: "The buck stops here."

A Girard Self-Reliance Technique

When I give a lecture, I'm usually introduced from the platform, but I come running up from the back of the room. Every time, I suddenly realize I'm up there alone, standing on my own two feet. How do I handle it? First, I take a deep breath, then I pause to look around.

This is the first time I'm meeting these people. It's also the first time they're meeting me. I've heard a lot about them. They've probably heard a lot about me. I ask myself, Can I win them over? I realize the reason they're there is that they want to be won over. I realize that we're on an equal footing—Joe Girard and the audience.

When you are on an equal footing, you are no longer lonely. Your self-reliance grows by leaps and bounds. But self-reliance, like any muscle, must be exercised to remain strong. You'd think that once I handled a lecture situation, all the others would be no problem. Not true. Each new time I have to begin the process all over again.

Tough It Out

Some years ago Ruth McKenny, a newspaper columnist from Ohio, went to Manhattan with her sister. She wrote about their many misadventures in a series of sketches for *The New Yorker*. Later they were made into a hit play called *My Sister Eileen*, and even later into a Broadway musical called *Wonderful Town*. In it, Ruth sings, "Why-oh, why-oh, why-oh did I ever leave Ohio?"

That classic Ruth-Eileen musical comedy is a favorite of Muriel Siebert, a woman who is an outstanding example of someone who had to stand on her own two feet. Ms. Siebert sings no song of regret. "I left Ohio in my twenties," she says. "I had a beat-up Studebaker and $500 in my jeans. It was one of the smartest moves I ever made in my life."

Muriel Siebert—friends call her Mickie—has made a lot of smart moves in her career, but maybe the smartest was to establish her own business. Today that business is Muriel Siebert & Co., Inc., in New York City, one of the most successful discount brokerages in the country.

From the $500 "in her jeans," she has come a long way. She now owns a seat on the New York Stock Exchange. Indeed, she was the first woman to own a seat on the Exchange. Siebert is referred to as "The First Woman of Finance." But how did she reach those heights? By realizing that others in a male-dominated business were not going to let her "join the club," and that she would have to start her own business and stand on her own two feet.

When Siebert arrived in New York from Ohio, she landed a job as a $65 per week trainee in research at a brokerage house. (She took that job instead of one paying $75 in accounting.) She became an industry analyst. At that time, senior analysts were allowed to "dump" an industry on a new trainee. Some that were dumped on her proved pure gold, not the dogs that senior analysts might have thought. She wrote reports in the field of airlines, from the analyst who covered railroads, shipping, and all other transportation. "If it moved," she grins, "I tracked it!" Soon other senior analysts gave her other industries: radio, motion pictures, and television. She followed those companies' performances as well and wrote reports on them.

At that time, she was not registered to sell stocks. Then, while working at another brokerage firm, she received a call from a company for which she'd done research. The company told her that, based on a report she had written, they had made money. They told her they owed her an order. Her first order. Siebert was registered in a hurry, moving out of research and into buying and selling stocks for clients. She went off salary and onto commissions, ultimately linking up with a series of small firms as a partner.

Siebert wasn't satisfied. When she tried for a partnership in a major brokerage, she was rebuffed. But she was a Buckeye, and she refused to be disregarded because, as the truth soon struck her, she was a woman. There'd be no more "working for" or "working with" bosses or partners. She would go into business for herself. Her advice to herself then, as well as it is to others now who want to start a business, is simply, "Go for it!"

She couldn't afford an office, but a firm she had done business with offered her a corner in their boardroom. In that corner, she found herself alone. In whatever direction she turned, she faced only herself. It was scary. She knew that standing on her own two feet was going to be tough, especially in the competitive business of buying and selling stocks, assuming she could find clients. Find them she did.

If the going was tough, then she'd tough it out. She knew she could do it. She recalled the day her father, a dentist, had died broke from a long bout with cancer. She knew her father would say, "Mickie, tough it out!"

So scrappy Mickie Siebert toughed it out in that temporary office. She borrowed $300,000 from a bank and, although there was a great deal of resistance on the part of others, she bought her own seat on the New York Stock Exchange for $445,000. Within six months she was out of the boardroom and into a fine office of her own. Off and running, Muriel Siebert & Co., Inc. grew into a multimillion-dollar company.

Muriel Siebert served for five years as the first woman superintendent of banking for New York State. She ran for the U.S. Senate in New York, but did not get beyond the primaries. She has received honorary doctorate degrees from eight colleges. Along the way, did she make waves! It did not faze her that she had been turned down by nine of the first ten men she asked to sponsor her application for the Exchange, or that Wall Street seemed determined to give her the cold shoulder.

If you were to ask Muriel Siebert how to stand on your own two feet and stay there, her answer would be: "Don't be afraid to take risks or to take a stand. And whenever someone or something tries to knock you off balance, tough it out!"

Why-oh, why-oh, why-oh did Mickie Siebert leave Ohio? Because she was confident in herself. She had the determination to "go for it!" It was the first big step she took as she mastered her way to the top.

When You Fall Down, Get Up!

"When you're a baby, the time comes when you get up from your hands and knees and start walking. You fall down. You get up. Finally you stay up. You're standing on your own two feet." That's Anthony Sorrentino speaking. He's a model of self-reliance. Born in Marsala, Sicily, he came to the United States when he was fourteen. Fate and politics prevented him from arriving on U.S. shores at an earlier date.

I've known Anthony for years. I bought suits and brought them to him for alterations. He was then and is now a successful tailor. Anthony Sorrentino is also the owner of four tuxedo rental shops that do a thriving business. He even supplies competing rental shops with tuxedos and formal wear. Weddings throughout the year provide heavy demand, and during high school and college proms, the stores are really jumping.

But it was not always like that. Anthony's father is Italian, his mother is a U.S. citizen by birth. After World War II, his mother wished to bring him to America. The papers were readied, the arrangements were made, everything was scheduled. There was just one hitch.

Italy, during its first opportunity since the war to have free elections, was urging everyone to get out and vote. Anthony's mother, in the spirit of the moment, did what she felt was her civic duty. She voted. That was a mistake. When a U.S. citizen votes in a foreign election (or serves in a foreign army), his or her citizenship is in jeopardy. Shortly after the election, his mother received word from the U.S. government that she would not be allowed to come to the United States with her son.

In Sicily, Anthony had been apprenticed to a tailor at the age of seven. He received no pay; compensation came in the form of "learning how things are done in a tailoring shop." After seven years of apprenticeship, he received permission, along with his mother, to come to the United States. His father and the rest of the family emigrated a little later.

Anthony had always been self-reliant, although he didn't think of himself that way. The family came to Michigan. Anthony enrolled in high school and, after school, he went to work in various tailoring shops. Then, when he was sixteen and in the ninth grade, his father was hurt at the factory where he was employed and could not continue working. Anthony quit school. He was an honor student and his teachers urged him not to drop out.

"I've got a family that I need to help support," was his answer. He was on his own. He got a job at $37 a week, but that didn't help out very much. At eighteen he decided to go into business for himself. His father had some savings, and for $3,000, Tony bought a tailoring business. He owned it for two years, then sold it.

Standing on his own two feet had been rough. For a while, he worked at other tailoring shops. Then, for a second time, he decided to establish his own business. With his brother and several other partners, he bought a clothing and tuxedo shop. He had $80,000 invested in inventory, then a number of events occurred that seemed to say: "You can't make it on your own. Give up the idea." Consider:

- The night before he was to open for business, thieves broke in by cutting through the wall of a shop next door. That night $80,000 in inventory was blown away.
- The store was restocked, and then it burned down.
- A fraudulent insurance agent had not given Anthony's initial premium check to the insurance company. There was no record of insurance.
- An important witness to the extent and value of the store's inventory died.

Anthony, as they say, had had it. He went to work for other tailor shops, but it wasn't long before the desire to own his own business was again spurring him on. He had always believed, "You fall down, you get up, you're standing on your own two feet."

This third time he opened a custom tailoring and tuxedo rental shop with his brother-in-law, but to truly stand on his own, he soon bought out his brother-in-law's share. He decided to listen to others, but in the long run he made sure he made his own decisions. If he fell, he'd fall on his own. If he rose, he'd rise on his own. He thinks of the song that goes, "Pick yourself up, dust yourself off, and start all over again."

"That song could have been written about me," he says. "That's the only way, at least my way, to develop self-reliance." Sorrentino mastered his way to the top of his profession. Today, Frank's Tuxedo Rentals claims a healthy share of the Detroit metropolitan market.

Frank's?

That's right. You won't find him operating under the name of Anthony Sorrentino. He picked the name "Frank's" out of several in a hat. He believes it has a nice stand-on-your-own-two-feet ring to it. So do I.

Realize You're Not Alone

"I realized one day that no one cared, that I was all alone." That's how Judith Briles put it when she started her own business. She knew it was time to tap her inner reserves and stand on her own two feet.

At one time Briles was a successful stockbroker for E. F. Hutton. In the late 1970s she decided to strike out on her own. Despite the realization that she was "all alone," she established the Judith Briles Co., and built it into one of the most successful businesses involved in financial planning.

Then she decided to start anew. Fresh fields. Like myself, she decided to master her way to a different top. By 1986 she had already published two books, *Woman's Guide to Financial Savvy* and *Money Phases*, but she decided to leave her successful company and form what is a veritable whirlwind of a business.

Dr. Judith Briles, heading up the Briles Group, Inc., is a keynote speaker at business sessions and conventions, is a management consultant, is the author of eight books and numerous articles appearing in publications like the *Wall Street Journal*, *USA Today*, and the *New York Times*; and has her own radio and television talk shows in Colorado. Nationally recognized as an expert on women's issues, she has been a frequent guest on

Good Morning America, *CNN*, *Oprah*, *Donahue*, and the *Joan Rivers Show*.

On first talking to Dr. Briles, one might get the impression that she is *all* business. She is a businesswoman. She is a business in herself. She is tough, hard-hitting, self-driven. All true, but there is a vulnerable side to her. She has known pain and much sacrifice.

At one time she was deeply involved in fund-raising projects. One such project was to raise money for the restoration of old, historic buildings. The management group of one of those projects grossly mishandled the finances, and since she was the guarantee of the construction loan, she had to make good. She was propelled into managing a hotel, and in order to recoup money for the investors, she put the hotel into Chapter 11. The creditors got their money back, but she lost everything—nearly a million dollars in assets. In the middle of that mess, her son was killed.

A tough business woman? Yes. A sensitive business woman? Yes also. At times of adversity, of pain, she believes you have to recall the good things and dwell on them. She advocates writing them down. She believes in giving one's self a heart-to-heart talk to bolster self-reliance. She believes in keeping three things in sync: heart, head, and guts.

Dr. Judith Briles has mastered her way to the top in every field she's undertaken. To be able to do so, she has relied upon self-confidence. *The Confidence Factor* is the title of her Master Media seventh book. She developed the Ten Commandments of Confidence.

I have always believed that developing confidence in one's self is a necessary step in developing self-reliance. I believe that when it comes to standing on your own two feet you can't do better than following these principles of Dr. Briles:

1. *To your own self be true.* Listen to your inner

voice; don't let others derail you. March to your own tune, not someone else's. (Remember nonconformity?)

2. *Create positive thinking.* Associate with "energy chargers." Don't let negativism drag you down.

3. *Know that you're not alone.* Remember, millions of people have walked in your footsteps before you, and will do so after you.

4. *Learn something new.* Get busy, sign up for classes, read a book, get involved in your community. Whatever you do, it'll rejuvenate your brain cells.

5. *Assess the situation.* Be realistic. What would really happen if you lost your job, a bid on a contract, or if business got really bleak? (Tie this commandment in with the next.)

6. *Take credit for your accomplishments.* Pat yourself on the back. Keep a file containing all the complimentary things others have said about you and your work. Review it when things look bleak. In times of crisis, it's good to have such positive input at hand.

7. *Aspire higher.* Stretch yourself. Consider your role models in or out of your field of work. Read about them. Strive to be like them.

8. *Don't bottle things up; get some feedback.* Talk things over with those you can trust. Make sure the feedback you get is from someone who is caring, supportive, and nonjudgmental.

9. *Take care of yourself.* Eat right, exercise, sleep, play. Laugh a lot. Get your life in balance. Learn to make time for yourself.

10. *Keep in circulation.* When rough times or failures hit, it's common to withdraw, to not let the outside

world know that all's not well. The sooner you
reinvolve yourself, the sooner you'll get back on
target.

All or most of the above are universal principles. We've
touched on some of them in earlier chapters, but they bear
repeating. Dr. Briles lays them out, I think, in a tightly wrapped
package.

I'm struck by a theme that, for me, underscores Dr. Briles's
remarkable career: Adversity is a strong contributor to self-
reliance. She likes to quote former First Lady Eleanor Roosevelt:
"No one can make you feel inferior without your permission."

The Juice to Start With

Cathy Metry started her own business when she was desperately
in need of a job and with just $300 to her name. Today she
is president of the successful company she founded, AD-XL
Promotions, Inc. Those intriguing letters stand for "advertise"
and "excel." "If you advertise with us," she states, "you'll excel
and expand."

Formally, Metry considers her business as promotional marketing. Informally, it's an advertising agency that is completely
different from what most people think of as an ad agency. She
believes newspaper and magazine ads are too soon tossed aside,
and that radio and TV commercials are soon forgotten. But
Metry does believe in *planned* word-of-mouth campaigning.

Most businesspeople know that word-of-mouth advertising
is one of the most effective ways of promoting a product or
service. For instance, I know that word-of-mouth by satisfied
customers was an important factor in my selling automobiles
at retail. Actually, many businesspeople see word-of-mouth as
something that just happens, without a promoter. For example,

a movie may be roasted by the critics, but if viewer word-of-mouth is "Don't miss it," then the movie can become a box office hit.

Instead of thinking of word-of-mouth advertising as something that may or may not occur, Cathy Metry and AD-XL make it happen. "I took the simplest idea—word-of-mouth advertising—and made a business out of it," she says. "We have been dubbed 'Walking Talking Billboards.' We give our clients a jolt of public awareness," she explains, "by praising their services in public places—for example, office buildings." AD-XL identifies a client's needs, then deploys its staff of personable people in selected locations to publicize those needs.

Clients range from nightclubs to restaurants, to beauty parlors. Often, AD-XL "walking billboards" are costumed in keeping with the business, and they literally stop passersby with "Have you eaten at so-and-so restaurant yet?" or "Here are a couple of free tickets to the opening of this comedy club." They work within a fifteen-mile radius of the client's business.

Actually, it was promoting a comedy club that gave Cathy Metry the idea of starting this different kind of marketing. The promotion was successful, and in the space of two years her business took off. "I had $300, and I invested it in my first client's word-of-mouth campaign. Within a week, I made $3,000." Any doubts on her part, any fears, were wiped away.

From her business, she now has an outreach in other states as well as in Canada and Europe. Her staff consists of full-time independent contractors, all of whom are people with distinctly individual personalities, yet Metry's business operates with a team concept.

The daughter of an automobile dealership sales manager and a real estate agent, Metry is a determined woman who will not take no for an answer. She is able to stand on her own two feet. She is persistent. She believes that "if you can see or talk to a potential client at least two times, you've created not only a client but a friend in business terms." Clients stay with AD-XL because of the personal relationships she builds—one that results in 100 percent business networking.

Metry believes in and maintains a positive mental attitude. Her office displays a PMA level graph that charts the relationship between the staff's positive mental attitudes and current volume of business. In building a business from nothing, Cathy Metry has mastered her way to the top by following these eight steps. They are also her guidelines for her AD-XL associates:

1. Be on time.
2. Be prepared.
3. Have a great attitude.
4. Don't lose your attitude.
5. Work your territory correctly.
6. Work your full eight hours.
7. Know why you're here.
8. Go the extra mile.

Although Cathy Metry has a college degree, she believes that you can start a business from scratch even without college. She quotes what she heard on the streets of Detroit: "It's all about a dollar, forget being a scholar." And she believes that "you get one chance to make your mark, so grab it. Think of things in the past that made you happy—your creative achievements—think about them positively, and you'll find your niche, your success."

From a very young age, she was determined to be in business for herself, to stand on her own two feet both in business and in life. Her philosophy is to smile often, maintain eye contact, stay enthusiastic, and always keep her promises. She believes that enthusiasm is the positive attitude that helps a person stand on his or her own two feet, and be confident and self-reliant.

Metry often quotes John D. Rockefeller, Jr., who said: "I believe in the sacredness of a promise, that man's word should be as good as his bond, that character not wealth or power or position is of supreme worth." Indeed, Cathy Metry's office, like my own, has many inspirational signs and quotations on the walls. All of them reinforce the team concept of AD-XL Promotions, Inc., and many of them refer to JUICE as a strong motivator.

The JUICE concept:

Join Us in Creating Enthusiasm!

I can't think of a better eye-opener than that.

A Refusal to be Pigeonholed

"They thought of me as a *black* public relations advisor, with solely black clients. Now everyone writes or phones me, and I'm a public relations advisor, period. A very fine public relations advisor. Color no longer has anything to do with it."

That's Terrie Williams, founder and head of the rapidly growing Terrie Williams Agency. The agency handles public relations for an impressive list of actors, singers, directors, producers, athletes, writers, and publishers. With offices in New York City and Hollywood, and with a full-time staff, the firm is the largest minority-owned PR agency in the entertainment industry.

In my book *How to Sell Yourself* and in my lectures, I've written and talked about overcoming prejudice. Terrie Williams not only is an outstanding example of a woman who has made a significant mark in the business world but she also knocked down any color barriers that lay in her path. Her techniques will surprise you, since they have nothing to do with confrontation or turning the other cheek.

Terrie Williams is a familiar name in the *New York Daily News*, the *Washington Post*, the *Boston Globe, Essence, Peo-*

ple, Hollywood Reporter, and many other publications. She has received numerous awards for her work in the communications field, and *Adweek* has cited her as a "Woman to Watch." She issues the "TWA (Terrie Williams Agency) Newsletter," and she's the author of *The Personal Touch: What You Really Need to Succeed in Today's Fast-Paced Business World*. In talking with her you can't help being both impressed and charmed by her down-to-earth manner, her warmth, her vitality, and her ability to put people at ease. I'd say that being a "people person" played a key part in her becoming so successful in her field.

Terrie Williams was born and raised in Mt. Vernon, New York, a town divided by railroad tracks. The north side was predominantly white, with well-to-do people; the south side, her parents' side, was predominantly black. Her parents were lower middle class—not poor—and they instilled in her a strong belief in the value of education.

Public relations work was not an idea whose time had come when she was a student at Brandeis and Columbia universities. Her chief interests at that time were clinical psychology and social work. The latter certainly was people-to-people work, but it was 180 degrees from PR endeavors. "I really care about people," she told me. With a master's degree in social work, she began training at Harlem Hospital and New York Hospital, and ultimately got a job with the latter. She was the only black on a large staff of medical social workers.

She counseled patients who were terminally ill, or who suffered from kidney failure, or who were drug-addicted, or women who had had several abortions. "There were a great many problems that I could never solve," she told me. "I was frustrated. There was a great deal of stress and strain in the job. It was obvious, too, that I'd never get wealthy in doing social work."

She decided to change her plans for the future. Today, she spends considerable time giving back and lecturing around the nation, and changing careers is one of the topics she often speaks about. Terrie believes strongly in controlling her own fate. She says her parents were most supportive of her independent spirit and her desire to achieve success. "If you don't assert yourself," she told me, "and if you don't *let others know who you are*, then you haven't got much chance of being recognized in any field. You must promote everything you do."

That boiled down to public relations, starting with herself. "I enrolled in a couple of public relations courses at the Y, which really whetted my appetite." Additionally, she learned more about PR work by offering to perform it, as a volunteer, to anyone who might use her services. She found takers, and in time she landed a job with the Black Filmmaker Foundation and, ultimately, as vice president of corporate communications for Essence Communications, which publishes *Essence*, a lifestyle magazine for black women.

She made contacts in the business, sports, and entertainment worlds. She bided her time, watching for the right opportunity when her ambitions and her desire for independence would be fulfilled by opening her own PR agency. She learned at a party that Eddie Murphy was on the lookout for an independent public relations person to represent him. She contacted Murphy and, doing a great PR job for herself, told him how she would promote him. The box office superstar hired her. Then the musician Miles Davis, Grammy Award–winning singer Anita Baker, and *Essence* soon became clients as well. Thus, in 1988, the Terrie Williams Agency was born and the rest is, as they say, history.

Because Terrie Williams is an African American, I asked her if she had an image problem, or faced bias when she started her PR agency. Did she see herself as a victim because of color then or later?

"Yes, there was bias when I started in business," she told me. "Before that, or later, I wasn't a victim. The bias was very subtle. I was pigeonholed. Because I was a black woman with major black superstar clients, people simply pigeonholed me.

The barrier was like being boxed in because of color. The knowledge that I could break out came when, just before I started my business, I asked Enid Nemy, a columnist at the *New York Times*, whether or not she felt race made a difference in what I wanted to do. Enid replied: 'Terrie, I never look at the color of a publicist. It's whether or not the people are doing *their* job in giving me the information I need to do *my* job.' I determined to be the best I could be and any color barrier would take care of itself."

That philosophy has made the Terrie Williams Agency a leader in the PR industry. "I refused to be pigeonholed as a black woman," she repeated. "Color, gender, economic status, are barriers only if you let them be. I determined to branch out, to get out of a specific arena. It takes time and it takes patience."

Whatever one's color, Terrie Williams offers these strategies:

- Perfect your craft.
- Never grow complacent. Take chances, explore opportunities.
- Keep networking.
- Assert yourself. Stand up for what you believe in.
- Never limit or pigeonhole yourself.
- Keep that knot of excitement in your stomach. It fires you up to do your best.

Terrie Williams's positive, upbeat, independent spirit comes shining through. "Be the best you can be," she told me, "and eventually people will recognize that and then nobody can deny you. Everything in life that goes around comes around, and everything that's supposed to happen for you, does."

Let Terrie Williams's strategies for mastering her way to the top be an inspiration to you in your own climb upward. I know they are an inspiration to me.

11
Commit Yourself to What You Want

E ARLY IN MY career I learned that mastering one's way to the top can never be a part-time job. Half-hearted efforts get you nothing. Heading for whatever top you're going after calls for a full-time commitment.

As I took the steps leading to success, I put forth not only a full-time effort but overtime. But that idea shouldn't make you feel as if you are suffering sticker shock when pricing a new automobile. Making commitments is something we all do. Some commitments are deeper than others, and some we have to struggle to keep, but whether easy or difficult, they all challenge us.

When we buy a home or lease a dwelling, when we purchase a car, when we take out insurance of any kind, we make a commitment to the mortgage payments, the rent, the car payments, or the insurance premiums. Commitments appear in other areas of our lives, too. When we marry, we commit ourselves to our spouses. When we bring children into the world, we commit ourselves to their raising and their support. When we sign a contract of any kind, we commit ourselves to living up to its terms. We commit ourselves to our families, our friends, and to the goals we set for ourselves.

Face it, you've made a commitment to master your way to the top. That means keeping all the agreements and promises you've made to yourself and to others as you forge ahead to reach success in the business world or in other endeavors. But there is an important consideration here: Commitments are stronger than agreements, just as agreements are stronger than promises. Their strength lies in the truth that life works when you keep your commitments to yourself and others.

If you feel that keeping your commitments is hard or impossible, then you might as well close this book and read no further. Nobody says that keeping commitments is easy. It takes a lot of willpower and self-discipline. But some of the things I've learned during my career, and the business success stories of others, may give you heart. As the song goes in *Damn Yankees*, "you gotta have heart."

Create Visual Reminders

Here are a couple of ways I used to stay committed to my goal of becoming a successful automobile salesperson:

First, at home, after putting in a day at the dealership, making presentations, giving demonstration rides, or enlarging my prospect file, I wrote down what I planned to do the next day. I listed no more than three objectives. For example:

- Make ten cold calls to drum up new prospects.
- During down time, call on people who couldn't come to the dealership for one reason or another, and try to sell them on their own turf.
- Work on my direct mail activities.

I never listed more than three objectives for the next day. It's easier to keep your commitments if you limit them to three.

And writing them down fixes them firmly in your mind. Your list becomes a visual aid.

Second, at the beginning of the following week, I'd refer to another visual aid—a phrase I had printed on a large file card and had thumb-tacked on the wall of my office. It read: "I'm going to beat last week's record!" Then I would start the process over again, listing three objectives I was committed to achieve the next day.

The visual aids reinforced my determination to keep my commitments. Many successful people might say that they have no trouble keeping commitments, that they don't need to list their daily or weekly objectives on paper. I say more power to them. Visual reinforcement worked for me. Try it; it could work for you.

Certainly there will be occasions when staying committed to your business or other goals will bring on periods of discouragement as well as moments of great satisfaction. It may often seem that for every two steps you take forward, you fall one step back. I know from personal experience that this can happen. But I never dwell on a backward step, for that only puts out negative vibes.

I found that staying committed was easier if I shared my satisfaction times with others. Doing so reinforced my efforts and gave encouragement to others. I also realized that sharing personal discouragements with others served no useful purpose. If you want to be successful, keep your troubles to yourself. Even if you're not having a good time at the moment, make people believe you are.

I gave that advice one time during a lecture. As usual, people came up afterwards to talk to me. One young motorhome salesperson said: "I've heard the expression 'crying on the inside, laughing on the outside.' Is that what you're suggesting?" I told him that was exactly what I meant. People have enough troubles of their own. Nobody wants to see your tears. Keeping them hidden calls for self-discipline. And self-discipline is one of the keys to keeping your commitments.

An Airline Ticket to Romantic Places

A remarkable woman used her past theatrical background to good advantage in starting a thriving business of her own. She had been on the stage since childhood, and now she is on a totally different kind of stage.

Kaye Britton was an actress and singer of exceptional talent. Her talent led to engagements in the theater, both on Broadway and on the road in the United States and abroad. She had played lead roles in *Song of Norway*, *Oklahoma*, *Carousel*, *Show Boat*, and *Bittersweet*, just to name a few. While in London, appearing in a production of *Gypsy Lady*, she met and later married George Britton, who was in the same production.

George Britton had a commanding stage presence. He was an actor and singer who succeeded Ezio Pinza on Broadway in *South Pacific*.

In time, Kaye and George started a family, something which sometimes—but not always—can cause a hitch in show business careers. "On the road" often meant "she was here, he was there." When one worked, the other might be, as they say in *Variety*, the theatrical newspaper, "at liberty." Kaye would be the first to admit that trouping is not the ideal way to raise a family, even though some performers had tried and succeeded. Too often, performers fail.

Decisions needed to be made as to goals and commitments. George and Kaye made the decision to put show business behind them, to forget the applause that came with the curtain calls. He went to work in the industrial theater department of a large midwestern audiovisual communication company. She got a job in the World Wide Travel Bureau of the Automobile Association of America. At last they could settle down in the same city and be a real family.

The couple still acted occasionally in community theater, but neither missed the bright lights of Manhattan, neither had regrets about leaving the professional theater.

Kaye was determined to be successful in her new career as a travel agent, but it was someone else's agency. Just as she used to fight for a good role in the theater, she now wanted to headline her own act. Kaye wanted to go in business for herself. She made a commitment to this goal and she never wavered from it. Clients she had served while employed in the AAA's travel bureau assured her that they would help. From their ranks two financial backers emerged to be silent partners; Kaye would, in effect, be on her own. She started Kaye Britton Travel.

Financial backing doesn't necessarily mean business success. Kaye Britton knew that there would be despair as often as there would be elation. For example, government deregulation, in her opinion, ruined the airline business, making it difficult to plan air travel for clients and serve them best in terms of reservations, schedules, and fares. Another blow was George's death after months of illness. He had always been there for her—helping out, encouraging her, providing support as he had always done from the day they first were on stage together.

Regardless of setbacks, Kaye never wavered in her commitment to succeed. What kept that commitment strong? Her considerable experience in the theater. "Every night," she explains, "I knew that my performance would be shaded by audience reaction. Every night and every matinee, the audience was different, sometimes intent, sometimes restless. I knew that I had to win over those audiences. I had to sell myself so they would believe in me and in the part I was playing, and trust me to not let them down."

How did she use that experience in her travel agency business? "All customers coming to a travel agency are different, just as theater audiences are different. My customers have different travel experiences in mind. Some know where they want to go and how they want to get there; others haven't the foggiest idea. All have different emotional needs they want fulfilled through travel. It may be a business travel for some people; for others, it's a way to find romance or adventure.

"I know I must sell myself first before I arrange a simple flight, a hotel reservation, or a car rental, or arrange something as complex as a round-the-world cruise. The one or two people sitting across from me is my audience. My desk is my stage. I must earn the trust of each new traveler. I just don't sell a cruise, for example; I make sure it is the right cruise for that customer in terms of people mix, ports of call, and their travel budget. How could I be bored?" Never being bored is another key to keep commitments.

Kaye Britton has kept her commitment to succeed: She mastered her way to the top. Since opening Kaye Britton Travel in 1980, she has built her business to where she and her employees serve a variety of commercial accounts as well as individual clients, couples, or families, whose leisure travel requirements receive equal importance.

Kaye Britton Travel is modest in comparison to Thomas Cook or American Express, but it is a success. Through ups and downs, peaks and valleys, Kaye extended her business around the world. And to know what's what in the great world beyond her agency, she travels a lot herself. Once again, as in her days of trouping, she is on the road. "There are a lot of reasons for my business success," she says, "but an important one is that I never once failed to keep a promise to myself or others, or an agreement with others." I call that commitment.

Fear Can Be a Spur for Keeping Commitments

I've written about and lectured on what I call the two most powerful words in the world: *faith* and *fear*. It's faith in yourself, in others, in your abilities, and in the future. It's fear that you can't do something that you've set out to do, or be someone. Fear of the past, fear of tomorrow, fear that you might fall on your face. Faith speaks for itself, but I've always considered fear a four-letter word that I try to erase from my thoughts.

There is always an exception to the rule, however—a time when fear can provide the boost that helps you keep your commitments. Such was the case with Martin Shoushanian, who founded and built VERSACOM, Inc. This company creates marketing communications programs for, but not exclusively, the Ford Motor Company. When asked what helped him keep his commitment to succeed with a small business of his own, Martin Shoushanian—usually called Marty by business associates and friends—replies with that four-letter word: *fear*.

Marty worked at the Ford Motor Company in its Merchandising Services Department. This was an internal profit center, part of the engineering staff. Profit centers must pull their own weight, producing their share of the company's overall profit objectives. The experience of seeing Merchandising Services make a profit served Marty later when his company relied on a healthy bottom line to survive.

Prior to his Ford employment Marty worked for a graphics firm. His experience there also served him well, since Ford's Merchandising Services handled in-house print operations for the divisions and interfaced with Ford Photographic, which also served the divisions.

Things seldom remain fixed, and Marty learned that nothing is as constant as change. Merchandising Services and Marty moved from division to division within Ford until the unit became part of the General Services Division.

Then, in the late 1960s, during the first big automotive crunch, Ford Motor Company eliminated its Merchandising Services Department of the General Services Division. The chill winds of change. Employees faced the familiar two options: stay within the company in some other capacity or leave. Marty chose to leave.

Another employee who had made the same choice started a company to handle print requirements in marketing communications for the same clients he had served when at Ford. Marty Shoushanian joined him in an association that lasted three years.

But Marty longed to have his own company, to achieve business success, to build an organization from its humble beginnings to its height of importance. He and an associate started VERSACOM, a company devoted to creating first-class materials for communications of marketing programs primarily through illustrated printed matter. VERSACOM continued to fulfill the same Ford and Lincoln-Mercury needs as had the Ford Motor Company's General Services Division years earlier. Then after thirteen years of operation, Marty bought out his partner. VERSACOM was now his alone.

Marty made a commitment to succeed entirely by his own efforts. He also made a commitment to his own philosophy. He expresses that philosophy in simple terms: "We do what we do because our clients give us the privilege of doing it. They expect from us top-quality work, delivered on time, and continuous service they can rely on." Marty Shoushanian states further that if he's not willing to provide quality and service, there's always somebody standing behind him who's ready to do it.

"That's something to be feared," Marty says. "At least I have that fear and as long as I've had it, it has only made me deepen my commitment to succeed. We are a service-driven organization. We strive to serve our clients as best we can and be honest with people in all our business dealings."

Fear of failure is another factor that strengthens Marty

Shoushanian's commitment to succeed. He cites the fact that his business is a reactionary one—a fire-drill operation. However, circumstances can go beyond a drill, and the real situation can result in a three-alarm egg on your face.

Working long hours and against time, Marty wrote and put together a computer-generated slide presentation for a client. He farmed out the production work. The client's presentation date was rapidly approaching. Then, disaster! The client's presentation time was moved up. Simultaneously the slide production company let Marty down, so that Marty wasn't ready. He blew the presentation, having put his client in an embarrassing, unsafe position.

As the saying goes, you're only as good as your last success. Marty feared the opposite: you're only as good as your last failure. That fear sharpened Marty's determination to succeed, to never be in that embarrassing position again. Setbacks like the botched slide presentation only reinforced his commitment.

Don't assume that Marty Shoushanian is fear-ridden, that he's a bundle of phobias. Far from it. But as he admits, there is never a shortage of concerns in his business—concerns about keeping his clients happy and satisfied, concerns about keeping employee morale high, concerns that his financial statement shows a healthy and prosperous operation. He simply uses fear in a positive manner—he makes it work for him.

And it does. The shelves showing VERSACOM's output is impressive: brochures, buff books, marketing pieces, "hot" sheets full of information for salespeople, press kits, and many others. To serve the diversified Ford Motor Company divisions— some of which are larger than many *Fortune* 500 companies— VERSACOM has a good-size staff augmented by freelance talent to provide writing and photographic support.

As president of this closely held company, Marty gives more than a 100 percent effort to his clients. And he expects the same from his staff and support people. Maybe fear is contagious—in a beneficial sort of way.

I still think of it as a four-letter word, but if fear might help you keep your commitment to master your way to the top, why not try it?

12
Associate
with Success

I 'VE LEARNED FROM experience—usually the best teacher—
that the road to the top can be potholed with associations of
the wrong kind. Also, your way can be paved smooth by knowing
the right people. That tried-and-true belief that people are
known by the company they keep certainly applies when it
comes to mastering your way to the top.

Who are the wrong associates? I'm not talking about lowlifes,
gangsters, bigots, tax cheats, liars, or spouse and child abusers.
I'm pretty sure you're not going to hang out with those types
anyway. I'm talking about people who are dangerous to your trip
to the top, as were stagecoach robbers in Wild West days. These
people get in the way of your progress. They hold you back.

Who are they? Well, first, there are the ATANA: the *All
Talk And No Action* people. Believe me, there are plenty of
those around.

They talk a good line, but that's all there is to it. They're
"wannabes," but they won't be because they do nothing. They're
easy to recognize regardless of where you work. Perhaps they
hang around the coffee machine or maybe they drift from office
to office with coffee cups in hand. Or they kill time by the
duplicating machine. Wherever they gather, they are ready to
share the latest gossip, to dish the dirt, but that's about all.

These people are bench warmers, not players, yet they bellyache because the coach (or superviser, foreman, boss, head honcho) doesn't put them in the game. Why should the coach do that? ATANA people don't score. In short, they are losers.

The sad part about losers is that they'd like you to be the same as they are. They envy any success you might attain. They're happiest when they can drag you down to their level. I guess it's because misery likes company. But worse, they represent the *F* word—failure. Sooner or later they fail, not only at work but also at life.

I've spent a great deal of time with these people in view and within earshot. I learned never to let them get in my way, and that's something you, too, need to learn.

The "Sad Song" Singers

Singing the blues? Leave that to experts like Ella Fitzgerald. The "sad song" singers I'm talking about are closer at hand.

Although they may not use these exact words when catching your eye or ears, the expressions on their faces speak just as loudly as the words they utter.

- "*Ah me*, I lost that sale."
- "*Alas*, the boss has it in for me."
- "*Woe is me*, I never have any good luck."
- "*If only* I had been around when opportunity knocked."
- "*What's the use*, I'll never get that contract."
- "*Trouble is*, competition has me beat."

Competition? If only the whiners and complainers realized that competition is good for you—it gets the juices flowing. Competition is what made American great.

The dealership where I worked as a salesman had the franchise for cars made by General Motors. At that time G.M. also had another division that manufactured and marketed appliances. I heard that at a product announcement meeting for appliance dealers and salespeople, a singer who pretended to be a salesman sang, "I've got the up-the-street, down-the-street, side-street competition blues!"

Well, I know all about competition. I had competition from salespeople in the same-brand dealerships in the marketing area. I had competition from salespeople who sold different brands of cars, foreign and domestic. More important, I had competition in the dealership where I worked—salespeople who operated only a few feet from me.

I loved it. Sad to say, although I looked at them as competitors who spurred me on to my best efforts, they saw me as standing in the way of their making sales. The truth is, they stood in their own way. Competition means you have to double your efforts if you want to beat it, and the whiners in life simply don't want to put in that extra effort.

Two instances come to mind, both affecting my business and where I conducted it. One was during the oil embargo. This political crisis really put a crunch on automobile sales in 1974. Gasoline prices climbed right through the ceiling and people put buying new cars on hold. I simply had to work twice as hard to make a sale. The "sad song" singers on the sales floor or the water cooler were saying "Woe is me, I can't sell cars during this crunch."

The second instance was when, in early 1974, all automobile dealers in metropolitan Detroit closed their dealerships on Saturdays. Now, Saturday was always one of the busiest days in a dealership. That was the one day people had off from their jobs and they could come in to look around and/or buy. I could see that no selling on Saturdays could really flatten my wallet—if I let it. Once again, the "sad song" singers were saying, "Poor me, I might as well give up if I can't sell cars on Saturdays."

The words *give up* are not in my vocabulary. I made up

my mind not to be influenced by, or even listen to, the bench warmers. They were making excuses when they should have been taking action. ATANAs. I rolled up my sleeves and went to work, which is one of the best pieces of advice I can give anyone who wants to master the way to the top. Oil embargo? Saturday closing? So what? I wish I could say I topped my record of 1,425 car sales in one year, which I had set in 1973. But I sold only 1,376 cars in 1974—49 car sales short! If you want to blame Saturday closings, it meant I would have made only one sale on each Saturday of the year, with three Saturdays left over. Those 1,376 car sales were a pretty good record after all. Where would I have been if I had listened to the negative attitudes of those excuse makers? Nowheresville.

By giving ATANA folks a deaf ear, I put myself in an atmosphere of confidence and self-assurance that could bring about only positive results. At that time, however, I was not aware of the positive effects of having the right atmosphere. It was not until some time later that I learned how atmosphere, or environment, can have a profound effect on one's attitude about business and about life—and that the resulting attitudes can actually determine one's actions.

Atmosphere, a Trigger for Success

"One of the most important factors in mastering your way to the top in business is to be in the company of can-do people." That advice comes from Richard M. DeVos, co-founder of the privately held AMWAY Corporation in Ada, Michigan.

Is there anyone in the world who is not aware of AMWAY? I doubt it. But for those who aren't, AMWAY is a leading manufacturer of consumer goods with a direct sales global network of more than a million independent distributors worldwide. Over 4,300 products—AMWAY's own as well as other brand names—

are marketed door-to-door and by mail order. Sales are in the billions. AMWAY's slogan is "We Deliver the Best!"

You probably had no problem surmising that AMWAY stands for the American Way, a way that exemplifies free enterprise, that recognizes people's right to use their God-given talents to make something of themselves through effort, determination, and faith. The business that DeVos started from scratch with his boyhood friend and lifelong partner, Jay Van Andel, markets its products throughout North America, Asia, and Europe. It's a business that employs 10,000 people worldwide. But before AMWAY was born, and at a very young age, DeVos learned just how important it is to associate with positive, upbeat, can-do people.

The son of devout parents, he attended a Christian school, which put him in an atmosphere of "God loves me, and I am a worthy person." The mood at the school was to be faithful and to study and learn. DeVos explains, "I hung around with kids who had that attitude, and who believed in the work ethic. Unfortunately, my marks weren't very good and my folks questioned whether they should continue to pay the expensive tuition."

So in his second year in the Christian high school he transferred to a public school. There the atmosphere was dramatically different. DeVos makes no value judgments as to whether things were good or bad; they were just different.

"After one year I went back to the Christian school. That was the first decision I knowingly made on my own, and it had a tremendous impact on my life." He believed then and does now that high school is when you settle down. Direction is established there. That's why it's important that the atmosphere be right.

The question was raised by his parents: "Who's going to pay the tuition?" DeVos said he would, but his parents paid it. Still, DeVos went to work. He found a job at a gas station as a pump jockey. He peddled papers. He worked long hours after school.

"The important thing," DeVos declares, "is that returning to the Christian school was the first commitment I had made as to the direction of my life, and I was willing to pay the price. I put myself back in an atmosphere of positive-thinking kids, kids who believed in themselves. This had impact on the rest of my life. I can never emphasize *atmosphere* enough."

I often ask people who have made something of their lives, who have fulfilled their dreams, "What sparks you as you go for the top?" When I asked DeVos that question, he referred to the sparks as "triggers"—triggers that bring about action of one kind or another: "We are often sparked or triggered by special events in our lives, things that are not self-induced. I was fortunate to be brought up in a family that gave me a can-do attitude. Such an attitude is developed according to the atmosphere one's in. There are events in life that one can't control. But atmosphere is something that's controllable."

DeVos developed and refined a philosophy that has served him and his partner well, and that I heartily recommend to anyone who wants to master the way to the top. He calls it the three *A*s: *A*ction, *A*ttitude, and *A*tmosphere.

Action

"We all wish in our dreams to take proper actions," DeVos is certain, "but we don't always. None of us do. All of us have weaknesses and shortcomings. The desirable action is just to do the right thing. But what gets you to do one thing vs. another? What gets you to prefer the presence of positive people as opposed to negative people? What gets you to stay in school instead of quitting school? What gets you to try a business of your own as opposed to never trying anything on your own? Taking action is difficult for some people."

Attitude

"There are factors in life that are not brought on by ourselves, though many times they are," DeVos explains. "Often they are very negative. There are calamities in life, and we just can't act positive when they happen and say, 'ain't it great?' That's just not realistic. Attitude is an important thing, and you can work on your attitudes, but you have to deal with the realities of life, with difficulties, world events, things beyond your control. Then what *do* you control that can increase your odds of developing a good attitude and take the right actions?"

Atmosphere

"That's controllable," adds DeVos. "If you work at placing yourself in an atmosphere of achievement, then you're more likely to have a right attitude and more likely to take right actions."

How did that philosophy trigger DeVos's success? While at the Christian high school he met his future partner, Jay Van Andel, a youth who shared DeVos's dreams, hopes, and goals. Together they planned to go into business. But first there was military service, which came on the heels of graduation. Through those days in the service the two young men received the love, support, and reinforcement of their parents. Yet that was about all they had with which to start a business.

DeVos and Van Andel started a little flying school and air service. Neither knew how to fly and their competitors were licensed pilots. Applying the controllable factors that determine proper actions, they wisely left the flying to others. "We could only focus on business, on getting customers," DeVos recalls. "Our competitors focused on teaching one person to fly. We focused on getting hundreds of people to learn to fly. We hired a dozen pilots to teach others how to fly. We focused on building a business." They have always focused on building a business.

DeVos and his partner eventually got out of the flying school operation and gave themselves a new challenge. In the late 1950s, they started a new business in a garage, an operation that was to become AMWAY. The business was selling a liquid cleaner, the forerunner of hundreds of household and personal items. The marketing strategy they devised for AMWAY was to build a complex network of distributors who found it profitable to sell to other distributors as well as directly to AMWAY customers. Today, Richard DeVos is a billionaire.

DeVos feels that too often people who dream of having a business of their own focus on the management of that business rather than on building it. Most businesses die, in his view, because the founder wants to become the manager of the business. "It's unfortunate," DeVos says, "that when a business one is building shows a little growth, that person begins to spend a great deal of time justifying the nongrowth. From that they slip into a blaming stage where they blame everyone but themselves."

There is no blaming, no finger-pointing at AMWAY. In mastering his way to the top, DeVos has always praised our American way as one that offers four important benefits to everyone.

1. *Freedom of choice*, whether at your job, or in school, or how hard you want to work, or whether you want to save your money or spend it.
2. *Reward for performance*, a great motivation factor.
3. *Recognition for achievement*, whether it's putting a kid on the honor roll or a bonus system used in business. Recognition is as great a driving force as financial rewards.
4. *Hope*, the fuel needed to reach great expectations.

DeVos believes that if you were not raised in a can-do atmosphere, the most important thing you can do is to accept the fact that you were not, then put yourself in an atmosphere of people who can be a source of encouragement. Too many people spend their lives hanging around with losers, therefore they think of themselves as losers. Associate with people who like challenges, who are positive thinkers, who are enthusiastic self-starters and hard workers, to reach the top in whatever field you choose.

There is a responsibility involved every step of the way. As DeVos explains, "If you enjoy the benefits of achievement, then you must put back some of yourself in time or energy or money to help those who, for whatever reason, can't measure up to be achievers."

In mastering his way to the top, DeVos has also helped millions on their way to business and financial success. He has never lost the personal touch. Indeed, he has made it part of his life to recognize and reward people for good performance. He has built his business on complimenting people, and he communicates with people in a uniquely personal way—notes. DeVos sends hundreds of notes to his employees and business associates. Each one is signed, "Love ya, Rich." Could anyone ask for a finer atmosphere than that?

Smoothing the Pavement

I believe that the road to the top is smoother when traveled with the right associates. Broom the wrong kind.

Who are the right kind? They are people who can help you. More important, they are people whose examples provide encouragement. Don't get me wrong. You won't get help from people if you try to apple-polish them or flatter them. They'll be on to you in a second; and you wouldn't want apple-polishers hanging around you. The key words are *associate with*, not *hang around*.

Now, who should you associate with? Successful people. People who have mastered their way to the top or who are on their way there.

Look for enthusiastic people. Optimistic people. People who see the glass half full, not half empty. The people who, as the saying goes, "when life hands them a lemon, they make lemonade." They are hard-working people—people who roll up their sleeves and tackle each objective on the way to the top.

You want self-starters—people who are motivated to succeed. Confident people, self-reliant and disciplined. People who willingly pass along what they know: teachers, trainers, supervisors, co-workers, older and wiser family members, coaches and leaders. All of these people can and usually are willing to smooth the way for you. They're successful people.

Association with success breeds success. One New Year's Eve at the Dunes Hotel in Las Vegas, I made a New Year's resolution. We all like to joke about how people break New Year's resolutions some twenty minutes after they're made, but this one I kept. My resolution was to be tough on myself, to associate with the right people and be successful, and to remember that mastering one's way to the top is a two-way street.

By that I mean if you hope to gain help from others, you must also be willing to give it. For example, I received help in my selling career from my general manager, Fred Murphy. He was more than a manager, he was my mentor. He told me what to do and what not to do. He pointed out the salespeople hanging around the water cooler—salespeople he called the "dope ring." They weren't drug users, just dopes. He warned me to stay away from them if I wanted to be a success. He was absolutely right. If anyone is responsible for my becoming the world's number one salesperson, it's Fred Murphy. I also received a lot of help from the new and used car sales managers where I worked, but it was Fred who pointed out to me the other side of the coin.

Just as you've been given help, give help to others. Following Fred's advice, I made it a point to help others in the dealership who were just starting out. I would say, "If there's anything I can do, count on me. Watch how I make a presentation, observe how I close a sale. Learn from me." Remember, you have to give in order to get. What goes around comes around.

13
What Did You Do Today?

CAN YOU GIVE a minute-by-minute, or even an hour-by-hour, account of how you spent the day? How much of your time was used wisely and productively? How much of the time you invested in business activity will bring you a satisfactory return on your investment? More important, how much of your time today was wasted?

Let's consider some facts about time. They'll help you when you feel like offering these excuses:

- "My, look at how time flies!"
- "I need more hours in the day to get my work done."
- "I don't have enough time for myself."
- "Time just seems to get away from me."
- "It can wait, I'll do it tomorrow."
- "I'm sorry, I'm running a little late."
- "I forgot what time it was, okay?"

Quit kidding yourself, friend. No one has any more or less time than you have. The president of the United States has exactly the same number of hours in a day. So does the man on the street. Everyone has 24 hours a day, 365 days a year. Throw in an extra 24 hours in a leap year. So you have 1,440 minutes in the 24-hour day. I call it the greatest gift of all.

The Gift of 1,440

When you realize that the time you have is neither greater nor less than that of others, the question then is not how much time you have for doing things but how you *spend* that time. Once you've spent that 1,440 minutes, it's gone. You can't spend it anymore. Think of yesterday as a canceled check; think of tomorrow as a promisory note—time you've got coming to you.

So success boils down to ranking those 1,440 minutes by priority. First things first. Tasks related to business or other work activities receive high priority, in order of their importance. Of course, if you give a task a No. 1 priority, don't give another task the same rank. If you give several tasks the same priority, your "first things first" approach becomes unglued. Worse, you lose whatever focus you had on your day's work. Keeping a sharp focus on what you need to do is an important step in mastering your way to the top. Being out-of-focus—like a blurred snapshot—simply weakens your ability to master your time. Your thoughts and ideas are liable to chase each other around in your head and take you nowhere.

Time-Wasters Rob You Blind

It's important to identify time-wasters. Here are some typical ones:

1. People dropping by your office to chat. (Learn to say no. After all, an office is a place of business.)
2. Lingering at the water cooler or the coffee machine

to exchange gossip. (Get your coffee and get
back to your desk.)

3. Writing lengthy letters and memos when a phone
call will do the job. (And cut out the personal
phone calls.)

4. Reading newspapers on the job, other than
newspapers and magazines that have a direct
bearing on your work.

5. Taking long three-martini lunches.

6. Taking too many coffee breaks.

7. Offering long-winded explanations. (Remember,
being brief and to the point saves time.)

8. Letting meetings run on and on. (Start on time and
finish on time.)

9. Putting things off until tomorrow. (Finish what you
start and don't go home before you're finished.
Tomorrow may be another day, but it's *today* that
counts.)

All of these time-wasters take a big bite out of your 1,440
minutes a day.

Getting Organized

Time management people suggest organizing one's time by
breaking the twenty-four–hour day into three broad segments:
eight hours for work; eight hours for leisure (eating, travel,
entertainment, etc.), and eight hours for sleep. Often work hours
overlap into leisure hours, and leisure hours sometimes rob
hours from sleep—that is, unless you take control of your time.

I have four rules concerning time, which I call my Four
Rules of Life:

1. *When I eat, I eat.* I don't allow mealtime to be

disturbed by matters better handled during other times.

2. *When I sleep, I sleep.* I love to sleep. Again, I don't let my sleep hours be disturbed by nonsleep activities.

3. *When I play, I play.* I never mix work and play. I closed my car sales in my dealership office, not on a golf course or a handball court.

4. *When I work, I work.* During those work hours, which are a measure of business success, I don't waste my time; and I don't let others waste my time, either.

By following these four rules, especially rule no. 4, I am in a better position to make every minute count.

Of course, the closer you get to the top, the more you are able to manage your time. On the way up, however, supervisors and others will control some of your activities, assigning you tasks with start and completion dates. Many books have been written and many seminars have been held on time management. There are many techniques. But if you follow the simple ones in this chapter, you'll know all you need to know about controlling your time.

Making Time Work for You

"Everything I do is carefully structured. Otherwise I could never accomplish anything," according to Art Van, chairman and CEO of the Art Van Furniture Company, which operates nearly a score of furniture stores in Michigan. The overall size of the business, its facilities, and its sales volume mark it as being one of the largest furniture operations in the country. Art Van employs hundreds of men and women who, like himself, are dedicated to customer satisfaction and to meeting people's furniture needs. "I love people," Van states. It shows in his operation, which not only is a furniture business but a people business as well.

Art Van has successfully mastered many important techniques and steps on his climb to the top. Among them is an important technique for using time to the best advantage. When Van talks about "structuring everything carefully," his concept of "structure" includes prioritizing his activities, knowing what and to whom to delegate, and, most significant, managing time wisely and in the most productive manner.

In fact, Art views time as one of our greatest commodities and he deplores the fact, as I do, that so many people waste it. In today's terms, time is not recyclable. Being a clock watcher is nonproductive. Too few people view time as an investment. As with every investment, you want a satisfactory return.

The phrase "It's about time" has a literal meaning for Art Van. At a very early age—twelve going on thirteen, as he recalls—his father took him in hand. "Come on, kid," his dad said, "it's about time I take you out to get a part-time job."

Art was willing. Times were tough and Art really wanted to work. He wanted to learn how to sell, so his dad took him to a nearby merchant, an acquaintance, and said, "I'd like you to give Art some kind of job."

The merchant was hesitant. "Business is slow," he said, "the boy is young, and I'm not hiring."

"He'll work hard," his dad said. "He'll do anything—sweep the floors, clean things, whatever." Then he mentioned that what he and his boy wanted was to learn how to sell. He got the job, and since that day, Van declares, he has sold all his life. "I sold papers. I sold clothing. I sold furniture. I had a lot of drive and I was willing to put in the time to succeed." All of his selling was time well spent.

Like myself, Art Van grew up on the Lower East Side of Detroit. Believe me, it was a tough area. You had to be streetwise and a scrapper. Like myself, Art determined to make something of himself. And, like myself, his drive was sparked by a desire to prove to his dad that he was capable, that he could make it, that he could be successful. (One difference, however, is that his dad had faith in him whereas mine did not have faith in me.)

Art Van states, "My dad wasn't long on compliments, but he told me, 'Son, the sky's the limit,' and I believed him." For a while, as a young man, the sky was limited by military service. He came out of the army in 1949 and shortly afterward married his high school sweetheart. He still wanted to sell, and he did.

"I got a job in a furniture store, selling on the floor," he remembers, "and putting to use everything I had learned about selling at retail." He and his wife started a family. As the children were born (he is the father of ten kids), he doubled his efforts to succeed. "I became the manager of a store. I wanted very much to make a decent living for my family," he says, "so I knew I needed to make money."

Perhaps his father's words, spoken long ago—"Son, it's about time"—had a subconscious influence on him as he set his sights on the future. Time, he knew, was a precious gift to be used wisely. Indeed, during those early days he soon realized how important time was. "When you're working in a retail atmosphere and you're with customers, you have to make every moment count. You have to move along, qualify them, and close the sale. You can't waste time."

From then on, starting at age twenty-four, Art's years were marked by successes as well as setbacks that colored Van's philosophy as he took the steps to master his way to the top—to eventually own his own business. They were years of borrowing money and paying it back, of mortgaging his home, of enduring tough times in the late 1950s and early 1960s, of times without cash flow, of nearly going broke, of having partners at times then going it alone, and of selling stores and buying them back. All along, he followed what I've always preached. "I sold furniture," he states, "but, most important, I sold myself."

Finally, Art reached the goals he had set out to achieve—

nearly a score of stores and a huge warehouse to serve them. "I knew if I wanted to grow, it would be necessary to advertise. In doing so, I knew I had to get a geographical spread in order to gain the greatest benefit of newspaper circulation and of the radio and TV broadcast range." His stores blanket the metropolitan area. Art Van knew not only that it was important to advertise but the importance of where and *when*—timing.

As Art Van mastered his way to the top, he made time work for him. His principles of time management are extremely worthy. I urge people who are out to reach the top to follow those principles:

1. *Recognize the value of time.* It is the most precious gift, a pearl of great price. "Schedule meetings on a regular basis, and limit the length of your meetings," Van advises, "and make every minute of the meeting count. Also, I work by appointment only, and I expect people to be on time."

2. *Take control of the time alloted to you.* Use your allotted time wisely and productively. "Always remember," Van cautions, "to stay on top of things. That means staying on top of time."

3. *Establish priorities.* Go over your tasks. List what should be done at the beginning of the week and what can be saved safely until later. List what should be done at the beginning of the day and what can be handled at the end. "Prioritizing," Van states, "helps assure that you put first things first."

4. *Learn to delegate carefully.* Free yourself to do what are your primary responsibilities and pass on other tasks to assistants. "The more hats you try to wear," Van says, "the more time will slip away from you. Delegate, yes, but make sure—as I do—to delegate to top-notch people. That way you multiply yourself."

5 *Don't procrastinate.* It's true. Procrastination is
the thief of time. Never put off until tomorrow
what you should be doing today. "I made it a rule
to get the job done," Art Van says, "before I left
for the day."

We all know the adage "A penny saved is a penny earned."
It can also be said that "A minute saved is a minute earned."
Minutes and hours saved are time you've earned, and earnings
are what measure the return on your investment. I take my hat
off to Art Van.

The success story of this smart-working man is impressive.
When you move from one Art Van store to another, and look
over the extensive inventory of traditional, contemporary, and
trend-setting furniture, you see the reflection of a man who has
mastered time, as he mastered his way to the top.

Some More Timely Tips

Art Van uses many of the time-management tips I have offered
in my books and lectures, but he uses them in a slightly different
way, and that's fine. You, too, can do the same. Adapt the
techniques and principles to your situation—your job or profession, your class schedule if you're a student, your teaching
assignments if you're an instructor or a professor.

Earlier I mentioned that tomorrow is a promisory note—
time you've got coming to you to spend wisely. How would you
like to fatten that amount of time in a way you may not have
thought of? How would you like a free month every year, without
rearranging the calendar?

Come to work each day an hour earlier than you usually
do. I did this during the year I sold 1,425 cars at retail, and I
continued to do so for as long as I sold automobiles. By coming
to work earlier five days a week, you gain five hours for work.

That totals more than 250 hours per year. Get out your pencil and divide those hours by 8—the normal number of hours in the workday—and you come up with thirty-one days—an extra month in the year.

Consider the results if you stay an hour longer at the office every day. That would give you another extra month. How can people complain that time gets away from them when they have at their fingertips the ability to gain one or two extra months a year?

Get to work at once on managing your time in the most effective manner. As the old saying goes, It's later than you think.

14
The Importance
of Honesty

I T CANNOT BE said often enough: Be absolutely honest in all
your dealings. Never cheat if you want to master your way to
the top. Never lie. Lies—even little white ones—have been
responsible for more people tumbling fast from whatever tops
they were trying to reach or had already mastered. How big a
fall can that tumble be? Consider the tragic example of how a
lie to the American people brought about the resignation of a
U.S. president.

It's a sad but true fact that children lie to their parents,
parents lie to their children, spouses lie to each other, trusted
officials lie to the people. Adolf Hitler said, in effect, if you tell
a lie, tell a big one, and the more often you repeat it, the more
people will believe it.

Yes, telling and repeating falsehoods is commonplace. But
you don't want any part of such practices. No way.

Many stories have come down to us through the years
concerning honesty and dishonesty. Some of the stories are
true, others have become legends. Nearly every child at school
learns the story of George Washington and the cherry tree.
When George's father confronted him and asked who chopped
down the tree, young George, holding up his little hatchet, said,

"I cannot tell a lie. I did it. . . ." True or not, it makes a nice story. It's one of the first I learned as a kid.

Every child at school also learns the story of Abraham Lincoln who, as a young boy, was sent to the store by his mother. It was some miles to the store. On the way back, young Abe saw that the storekeeper had given him too much change. The boy trudged all the way back to the store to return a penny or two, so the story goes. The amount of money isn't important, but the honesty Abe showed is. It's a worthwhile example.

More recently, President Franklin D. Roosevelt told Americans the truth when he said, "The only thing we have to fear is fear itself." It helped people get through the Great Depression.

Winston Churchill, England's prime minister, never lied to the British in World War II, as Nazi bombs plastered their nation. He promised them it would take "blood, toil, tears and sweat" to defeat the enemy. As the popular song goes, he "never promised them a rose garden."

I'll be grateful all my life that my mother taught me the value of honesty. She was a woman of honesty. The greatest truth she gave me was to assure me, "Joey, you can be somebody, you can make something of yourself." I put her faith in me to work as I began my career in selling. I never lied about the vehicles I sold or about myself. It earned me the trust and goodwill of my customers. If I had not been honest and above-board in my work I wouldn't have been able to sell ten cars, let alone 1,425 in one year.

The Good Book says to tell the truth and the truth will make you free. Free from what? Free from guilt, shame, mistrust, gossip, scandal, and loss of pride. And here's an important truth: When I say to you, in lectures or in books, that you are number one, I am being absolutely honest. You *are* number one!

And when you face a mirror and tell that to yourself, you are being honest with yourself. Who better to tell the truth about yourself than you? For one man and his formula for reaching the top, absolute honesty in all his dealings was one of the most important among his steps to success.

Victor Potamkin's Five-Step Formula for Success

Some auto dealers believe that owning a single, profitable dealership spells success. They're right. Others believe that owning two, even three, money-making car dealerships marks them as having reached a plateau in the business world. If that's the top they want, they're right, too.

But having a chain of over fifty dealerships makes a dealer a super success in my or anybody else's book. Victor Potamkin is a super success story. He heads a mega-chain of fifty-plus dealerships stretching from Manhattan to Miami.

Certainly Potamkin is one of the biggest, if not *the* biggest, auto dealers in the world, with sales in excess of $1 billion a year. Sons Alan and Robert supervise the bulk of the Potamkin new and used car sales, and parts and service operations, from Miami and Philadelphia, respectively.

Victor Potamkin's career could be the basis for a Horatio Alger book. He mastered his way to the top from a beginning so humble that it would seem almost impossible to make it. His parents operated a small fish stand. Although they were very poor, they also were quite supportive of Victor in his efforts. "I was very young," Potamkin states, "when I got a job driving a delivery truck for eighteen dollars a week. I delivered poultry and other meats." This was before World War II.

Potamkin says that he noticed people had definite likes and dislikes when it came to poultry. Some folks like white meat from chicken, others liked the dark. He was the first to decide there would be a good profit in selling cut-up chicken in addition to the whole bird. "Why not sell the white meat to those who preferred the white, and the dark meat to those who wanted the dark?" So he opened a store and devised a new advertising campaign, creating the slogan "Be smart, Buy a part." To highlight his new concept, he put a man in the window of that store so passersby could see the chickens being cut up and know that they were fresh. It proved to be ingenious, and even though chicken sold for only a few cents a pound in those days, he made money. His secret was high volume and low prices.

After the war, Potamkin thought about opening a store in Florida, but his brother made him aware of an automobile dealership that was available in Pennsylvania. Potamkin acquired that dealership, which was in Philadelphia, and he has been an auto dealer ever since. His secret of success in this new venture was high volume and low prices!

From that beginning in the City of Brotherly Love, Potamkin made selling automobiles and auto parts a family-operated affair that has expanded through the decades. "Since I was a young man," Potamkin says, "I followed five important principles. They've always worked for me, and I believe they're responsible for the success I've enjoyed."

This is Victor Potamkin's five-step formula:

1. Choose a business you enjoy and a product you can be proud of. This will make the inevitable hard work and problems seem a joy as well as a challenge.
2. Expect hard work and problems.
3. Always be prepared with a plan B. How well you handle that alternate solution will spell the difference between success and failure.
4. Build long-term market share via customer satisfaction and repeat business. Be absolutely honest in all your dealings.
5. Pay employees on an incentive rather than a salary

basis and allow key managers to become
partners in the company they control.

Although the many Potamkin dealerships, selling both domestic and foreign-make vehicles, make up a family chain, all
of the stores have partners on the premises. Some operators
have as little as a 20 percent share in a Potamkin dealership;
others might have a much larger partnership share.

Always looking around for new opportunities (such as his
transition from chickens to automobiles), Victor has also become
owner of a chain of radio stations and an ABC-affiliate TV station
in Palm Beach, Florida. "Opportunities are all around one," he
states.

"People are my spark," he explains, "and we make sure the
people who work with us are satisfied and do well." Then he
adds, simply, that all the people in his dealerships, his family
included, have one other important partner. "The customer is
a partner with everyone."

With that philosophy, is it any wonder that Victor Potamkin
rose from a delivery truck driver to become the biggest automobile dealer in the world?

That Magic Number 250

Regardless of your goals, regardless of your line of work, if you
want to master your way to the top as I have, and as Victor
Potamkin has, consider the following questions:

- Do you have a product or do you perform a service
  that you can be proud of and that others can trust?
- Are people your spark? Do you treat others as you
  would like to be treated?
- If you operate a business, are your customers your

partners? Is your end goal one of customer satisfaction?

• Most important, are you absolutely honest in all your dealings?

Think of Girard's Law of 250: The way you interact with people, the way you treat them, will be multiplied 250 times. I've seen the Law of 250 at work time and time again.

Why 250? It's a magic number I learned from a funeral director who knew the number of memorial cards he should order for someone's funeral. Experience had taught him that 250 people could be expected to show up at the average funeral or memorial service. I learned later that restaurants and lounges also expected an average of 250 to show up each evening— not mom-and-pop operations, of course, but larger dining rooms and cocktail lounges. I usually include the Law of 250 in my lectures.

How does the Law of 250 apply to your words and actions? I took to heart what the funeral director told me, and did some arithmetic on my own. I jotted down the effect of word-of-mouth over a specific period of time—in my case, a month of selling. To my amazement it turned out that 250 people would hear the good or the bad and act upon it. One person would tell two others, those two would each tell two others, and so on. Alternatively, one dissatisfied customer could, in time, result in 250 dissatisfied customers.

If a dishonest remark or action to one person can reach the ears of 250 others, think how devastating that could be as you master your way to the top. On the other hand, consider how that same law can work to your advantage when you are honorable, truthful, and aboveboard.

Don't Just Stand There, Buy Something!

At least one person has seen that unfailing Law of 250 work to his benefit again and again. Honesty meant so much to him that he added *Honest* to his name.

"Don't Just Stand There, Buy Something!" was typical of the signs that urged shoppers to come in and buy merchandise at bargain prices at Honest Ed's store at the corner of Bloor West and Markham streets in Toronto, Ontario, Canada. Honest Ed's is an amazing store that has turned Ed Mirvish from a dirt-poor high school dropout into a millionaire many times over. And that is no exaggeration.

The remarkable success story of Ed Mirvish includes his ownership not only of a very unique merchandise mart but of the Royal Alexandra Theatre in Toronto, the home of many hit shows and musicals, and the showcase for some of the most famous headliners in North America. He also owns the Old Vic Theatre in London, England, known as the most famous theater in the world. Vaudeville to Shakespeare—Ed has seen it all.

Add to that his restaurant, Ed's Warehouse (because he designed and carved it out of an actual warehouse). Actually, there are a half dozen dining rooms in Ed's Warehouse, offering a variety of menus in surroundings filled with antiques. With over 2,600 seats it's a money-maker. Ed puts it this way: "Hey, it's one of the most successful restaurants in the world."

Ed is known for his enthusiasm. And when he states something is a success, you can bank on it that he's been absolutely honest. That's Honest Ed.

Success is a word that goes with Ed Mirvish, like Canadian bacon goes with eggs and like a game of darts goes with a nice, friendly neighborhood pub. How did Ed's success begin? From scratch. Ed's parents emigrated from Russia and Austria to Baltimore, Maryland. His father tried his hand at a number of things, including a saloon and a pool hall. He sold encyclopedias. He owned a grocery store. Ed explains, "My father wasn't exactly a loser, but he wasn't a winner, either. Above all, he was a fine man."

The family moved from Baltimore to Washington and then to Toronto when Ed was not quite ten years old. His father opened a grocery store in Toronto, and there young Ed received his first lessons in retailing. To help pay the bills and to save money, Ed's parents not only lived in rooms behind the grocery store, they also rented out a couple of rooms above the store.

Ed worked hard at the store. He waited on customers, he picked up merchandise from suppliers, he developed muscles from lifting heavy crates, and the way he biked all over the neighborhood delivering groceries, you'd think he was in training for the Tour de France.

The family was poor. There wasn't even enough money to bury Ed's father when he died, so the Masonic lodge to which his father belonged took care of things. Ed had to drop out of school at fifteen so he could take over the grocery store. During nearly ten years of struggle, experience sharpened his skills at buying and selling produce, being his own accountant, and trying out different ideas of merchandising. Despite his honest efforts, Ed kept the store going almost by the skin of his teeth. It just didn't seem to earn a thin Canadian dime.

Ed realized that his dad's way of operating, which he had followed to his regret, was a losing proposition. It was a mistake to hand out credit to anyone who asked for it, always offering more and more credit, so that he wound up with a fistful of bills most customers couldn't pay. His absolute faith in others hurt him, and the day came when he called it quits. "Hey, I was beginning to think that Leo Durocher, the Brooklyn Dodgers manager, was right when he said nice guys finish last." I don't think Ed really believed that, however. He told me his honest dealings did pay off. He learned what *not* to do in retailing—

namely, don't sell anything on credit, either in person or on the phone.

Desperate for work, Ed found a job in a supermarket, and that experience, too, helped him in retailing. "In my spare time," Ed told me, "I got involved in other operations. Would you believe a dry cleaning shop on the same premises of my dad's former grocery store?" No, I didn't find that hard to believe, knowing Ed. I just found it amazing that Ed, always busy, always on the go, always running, had any spare time.

Ed always wanted to be in business for himself. That desire runs through the majority of success stories in this book. Ed wanted to be answerable to no one. He wanted his energy to pay dividends only to himself. Two important things happened around that time: He got married and he and his wife opened a small shop where Honest Ed's now stands. It was a dress shop, and both he and his wife put in long hours. He would buy dresses at wholesale and sell them at retail for double the price. That 100 percent markup began to change his fortunes because his prices were still bargains. All this sounds like Ed Mirvish worked a plan toward success and I believe he did, although he states it differently.

"My success has really been a development or involvement," he told me. "It started with being hungry. When I was hungry, the first thing I wanted to do was eat regularly. Once I was making a living and not just scratching it out, my family and I never wanted for food on the table. I started that small store in Toronto with $214 many many years ago. Everything grew and developed from that small dress shop."

Over the years he established and followed some important principles for selling. If the top you plan on going for involves owning your own retail business, you might be wise to adapt some of Ed's principles:

1. Be absolutely honest and aboveboard in all your dealings.

2. Cut all the red tape that you can from your operation.

3. Sell at bargain prices, and don't call it discounting.

4. Sell for cash only. Credit can leave you holding the bag.

5. Let people wait on themselves. This saves time and money, and it makes customers feel important.

6. Advertise and display to call attention, think wild.

7. Go for fast turnover in whatever you sell.

8. Don't do what everybody else is doing.

9. Expand sensibly.

In time, sensible expansion became possible for Ed. He eventually bought all the property adjacent to his store and the small shop became a block-long complex. It was not fancy—the floors were crooked, the stairways creaked, the layout was a bit like an obstacle course. But selling dresses expanded into selling a variety of items in seventeen different departments.

As always, Ed is completely honest about the way he describes his store: "Hey, it's a place where shoppers can save themselves a lot of money!" You can't be any more to the point than that. He decided to call his store Honest Ed's and claims he just happened to come up with that name by pure chance.

Pure chance? I am not so sure. He mentioned in passing that his dad was honest. He recalls that in his dad's grocery store there were honest weights beside the produce scale. Some impressions stay forever, and Ed is glad that they do.

Contests, publicity stunts, and marathon sales also helped Honest Ed's growth. No promotion was too wild, no idea for ads and slogans was too far out. Along the way there were ups and downs, of course, but as the years passed Ed Mirvish—the poor young lad who biked groceries all over the ghetto—made millions of dollars.

Ed doesn't measure success by the amount of money, the number of dollars, one has. "There are many measures of success to my mind," he told me. "Once you're making a living and you're not hungry anymore, then success is being able to do what you want to do, when you want to do it." And doing what one wants to do meant that Ed became a community-minded citizen, discovered culture, and became a patron of the arts. He bought for $215,000, and restored for $450,000, the famous Royal Alexandra Theatre, built in the early 1900s. Again, Ed is honest: "I was not a theater goer myself, but they were going to tear that beautiful building down and put a parking lot there. I didn't know anything about running a theater, but I couldn't see that Toronto landmark destroyed."

Ed didn't know anything about the restaurant business either, but he bought the property—a warehouse—next to the theater and opened up Ed's Warehouse Restaurant. "I figured that people who went to the theater liked to eat before or after the show, maybe both, so my restaurant made it easy for them." Extra easy, because diners are notified when curtain time is approaching.

Sometime later he acquired the Old Vic, the famed theater in London, and saw to its restoration: "When they were accepting bids for it in London, England, I submitted mine and it was accepted." One might think that the Old Vic is the crowning touch of his success story. Not so. Ed has built a new theater next to the Royal Alexandra, one that will house lavish musicals, built privately with his own capital. Also, he runs a museum that, he told me, is unique: "Everything in it is for sale, from five cents to $50,000 dollars. The women ask what can one get for $50,000; the men ask what's for sale for five cents."

From a kid with nothing to a man who has received royal honors from Queen Elizabeth II at Buckingham Palace, Ed Mirvish is shy, quiet, and unassuming. He's also a fireball. One thing he said to me with a big grin was, "Everything you've heard about me, read about me, Joe, is absolutely true."

There are many reasons for Ed's huge success, but I believe honesty heads the list. That, and one other important factor.

Ed Mirvish told me this: "The most wonderful thing about my success is the part that luck has played in it. Not the throw-of-a-dice kind of luck, but being lucky enough to be born in a country where opportunity to succeed is there for the taking. I say to all those I meet who are starting on their way to the top, 'How lucky you are!' "

Nothing but the Truth

Some years ago a hit Broadway play (that may have even played the Royal Alexandra) was called *Nothing But the Truth*. The plot concerned a fellow who, in order to come into a sizable chunk of money, had to agree to tell nothing but the truth for a period of twenty-four hours. Nothing but.

That may seem easy. In the play, of course, many obstacles test the guy's ability to keep from falsehoods. The point is that being absolutely honest and aboveboard, telling the truth and acting honorably, is not always easy.

In my book, hard as it may be, it's essential if you want to master your way to the top. If you slip, if you tell a lie—even a little white one—it's important to straighten things out as quickly as possible and try not to slip again. This chapter has touched on some important principles concerning honesty. Resolve to put them to work. At the same time, assume the role of the person in the play. It could be a tight fit.

15
A Quitter Never Wins

E very day we read about people who have gone into Chapter 11, who have declared bankruptcy. And we read about businesses that have done the same. You may know some that have. Chances are circumstances simply became too much for them. Declining markets, overexpansion, too many unpaid accounts receivable, little or no cash flow caused them to throw in the towel.

That is a blunt fact in the business world, and there's nothing disgraceful about declaring bankruptcy. Actually, it's a first step toward reorganization and starting over again. However, this chapter has nothing to do with bankruptcy in the financial sense. I want to tell you how to avoid bankrupting *yourself*— how to keep from falling short of the steps to success and failing to reach the top.

The moment you let down your efforts, when you fail to take one step at a time toward success, is the moment you find yourself short of what you need to get to the top. But you won't fall short if you never let up. Persistence pays off. Do your level best to keep from throwing in the towel. And don't let anyone else throw in the towel for you.

You all know how referees in the ring, or even a boxer's second, want to throw in the towel, want to stop the fight, even as the fighter struggles to get back on his feet. Sure, it's the referee's judgment call, but who's to know if the boxer, taking it on the chin, is ready to quit? As you master your way to the top there'll be many times when you'll be "taking it on the chin." When that happens, *don't quit*. Make that promise to yourself, and don't let someone else make the decision for you. When you hit trouble, change tactics. A boxer will back off a bit from his opponent and dance around a while, waiting for a new opportunity to close in.

Don't let the fact that I'm a salesman, a lecturer, and an author fool you. I'm also a fighter. When I was a young man I used to go to a lot of fights—Golden Gloves matches. In fact, I fought in the Golden Gloves tournaments in Detroit. Golden Gloves were some of the steps to the top that Joe Louis mastered as he went on to become heavyweight champion of the world. Back then I was influenced by trainers and boxing promoters who would say, "A quitter never wins and a winner never quits." I decided to make that philosophy mine because it was true in every sense.

The long-distance runner who gives up along the way might just as well have never entered the race. Persistence is what wins races. Air Force bomber pilots know that in warfare they have a mission. If they can't, for whatever reason, hit a designated target, they must be persistent and seek a target of opportunity. They know that a near miss is as good as a mile and equally nonproductive. So they keep at it to achieve the very best results they can.

Likewise, successful people are driven. Their success, most will admit, comes about because they persevere. They are persistent in their efforts to succeed. Indeed, sticking it out is the glue of success.

From Hell to Heaven in Five Days

There's a man who almost quit his life at age fourteen, then came back a year later to start a career that astonished the world. You sit across from him and you marvel. He's in his late seventies and he looks twenty-five years younger. The only thing broader than his shoulders is his friendly smile. His chest is big. His belly is flat and hard. His biceps bulge his shirt. He's called the Father of Physical Fitness.

He travels widely, he lectures, he appears before members of Congress, warning that something must be done for the health of our country. He's dead serious. He's Jack LaLanne.

Jack and I have been friends for years. We've appeared on the lecture platform together, but I've never told his story. He's been the subject of newspaper articles and magazine feature stories; he's received many honorary awards, including the President's Council of Physical Fitness Silver Anniversary Award; and his gym and his den walls are lined with photographs of him with some of the most celebrated people in the world. He's also published a half dozen best-sellers on health.

He is, of course, number one in my book for the way he's mastered the way to the top. His achievements are legendary. He swam the length of the Golden Gate Bridge in San Francisco, underwater, with 140 pounds of equipment including two air tanks. That's a world record.

At the time of our nation's bicentennial and to celebrate the spirit of '76, he swam one mile in the harbor of Long Beach, California, handcuffed and shackled, and towing thirteen boats, each representing one of the original colonies; the thirteen boats contained a total of seventy-six people. Is that patriotism, or what? Later, again shackled and handcuffed and pitting himself against heavy winds and strong currents, he swam from the Queen's Way Bridge in Long Beach Harbor to the *Queen Mary* a mile and a half away. This time he towed seventy boats with seventy people—an incredible feat.

He's done 1,000 chinups and 1,000 pushups in less than eighty minutes. Awesome. But those are just a few of the achievements of Jack LaLanne, now a respected businessman—in fact, a one-man business in himself.

How did it all begin? As he tells me, Jack was a sugarholic as a kid in kindergarten and upwards into his teens. Anything for a sweet. He was tempted by sweets, he was rewarded with sweets. By the time he was fourteen years old he was sickly, fifty pounds underweight and unable to participate in sports, getting failing grades in school; with an uncontrollable temper, he was a trouble-maker at school. Discouraged, even thinking of suicide, he dropped out of school. Popular? The girls wouldn't even look at him.

Then, at age fifteen, he attended a health lecture where he learned a simple truth. "I found out that if I obeyed nature's law," he says, "I could literally be born again." What was that law? Bluntly put, it was "Exercise and watch what you put into your body."

LaLanne was moved to action. He didn't aspire to be Mr. America; instead he said, "God, give me the willpower to refrain from eating the foods that are undermining my health. Well, my prayer was answered and I became literally born again." That was the end of foods that had no body-building characteristics. And that was the end of sitting around moping instead of exercising. Jack's habits and attitude did an about-face in less than a week. As he puts it, "I went from hell to heaven in five days."

He went back and finished school. At fifteen he joined the YMCA, mainly to use the pool and make a start at becoming an expert swimmer. He built a gym in his backyard. He had weights, a chinning bar, and climbing ropes. He started eating right—whole grains, nothing refined, everything natural, no emasculated processed foods, and he became a vegetarian.

He wanted to be strong and he wanted to be an athlete. Jack became captain of his high school football team and a champion wrestler. To cap it off, he bought a copy of *Gray's*

Anatomy to learn all he could about the wonder and workings of the human body.

In time, Jack had others working out at his backyard gym, including policemen who wanted to toughen up. They became his guinea pigs as he devised exercises. He could take the blubber off a fat guy and he could build up a skinny one. You'd think most people would find Jack's activities admirable. Yet at the time some people thought he was nuts because of the way he exercised and the foods he ate. To some he became a laughingstock. Lesser men might have quit the game, but not Jack La-Lanne. He knew a quitter never wins.

Instead, he went to Hollywood and worked in a few pictures. With the dollars he earned there, he came back to Oakland, California, and in 1936 opened the first modern health spa in the United States. He bartered memberships for paint jobs at the spa, for bricklaying, and for making patterns for his weights and exercise equipment that he invented. He invented the very first pulley machines, the first weight selector, along with the first leg-extension machine, plus other equipment. These concepts are the basis for much of the exercise equipment manufactured today.

That first spa has grown to nearly 100 franchised spas that bear his name across the country. Yet as he began that success story newspapers mocked him, doctors criticized him, even athletic coaches knocked him. But Jack didn't quit. His actions anticipated the growing interest in health and physical fitness in our nation and the emergence of spokespeople such as Jane Fonda, Richard Simmons, and Arnold Schwartzenegger, who have made workouts the daily routine of millions of Americans.

But at that first modern health spa, LaLanne realized he was going broke. People were not yet beating a path to his door. One day while giving a massage, he realized that if people weren't coming to him, he'd have to go to them. He started visiting high schools in the area to talk to young men. At first the students taunted him (their coaches had cautioned them that following

LaLanne could lead to athletic failure), but he persisted. He'd say to one of the fat kids: "How'd you like to get rid of that gut and get yourself in shape?" He'd pick a skinny kid and ask: "How'd you like to put forty pounds of solid muscle on your frame and go out for the football team?" That really caught their attention. To each who responded to his questions and who wanted to change his image, he'd say, "Give me your name, address, and phone number."

Then, at night, he'd visit the kids' homes, at their parents' invitation. He built up such home visits until he had fifty kids coming to his spa. He took off weight on some, put inches of muscle on all, and promised double their money back if he didn't fulfill his promises.

Soon Dads showed up, wanting to get back the flat bellies of their youth, and later the wives showed up wanting to get in shape too. Dads and Moms would say, "Don't tell anybody I'm coming." But word-of-mouth does wonders. The sneering stopped and changed to acclaim. And the acclaim has not ceased since. With it came television appearances and a health and fitness TV show that lasted for thirty-four years. In all those shows, the message was clear: Eat right, exercise regularly, and know that you're never too old to remake your body.

You know the question I always ask: "What sparked you on your way to the top?" Jack's answer is: "I wanted to be healthy and an athlete, and I wanted every man, woman and child to be healthy and physically fit, too." What challenged him? Kids who beat him up? People who sneered and criticized him? A desire to get even, to "show them"? His answer is simple: "No one challenged me. *I challenged myself.*"

Jack LaLanne's strategy for success is one that anyone who wants to master his or her way to the top can and should follow:

1. Make up your mind that you want to be the best.
2. Challenge yourself to achieve that goal.
3. Don't quit in the face of discouragement.

4. Push yourself to the limits.

Jack pushes himself and his body to the limits. He works out seven days a week. He changes his workout program every two weeks. He spends an hour or an hour and a half each day on weights. He spends an hour each day in the water, swimming in a pool beside the majestic California mountains. He has earned wealth and prestige. But more important than riches, he enjoys radiant health and enviable physical fitness.

Earlier, I mentioned achievements. I've saved this one for last. As most everyone has heard, escape from Alcatraz, when it was a prison, was considered impossible. But at age forty, Jack swam the treacherous waters from Alcatraz to Fisherman's Wharf in San Francisco, wearing handcuffs. At sixty—twenty years later—also handcuffed and with his feet shackled he accomplished the same feat, towing a half-ton boat. I asked him why he made that effort. He gave me the same answer he gave reporters at the time. He grinned mischievously: "To give the prisoners hope," he said.

The achievements of Jack LaLanne and the challenges he gave himself can bring hope to everyone who wants to master his or her way to the top. He will always be an inspiration to me.

16
Give Faith
a Chance

T HE MILLIONS OF people who have read my books and the millions who have heard me lecture know that I place great value on faith. I've written about religious faith and mentioned it in my lectures. You have your own beliefs and you follow them in your own way. I'm sure many of you rely on religious faith as you seek success in your profession or happiness in your relationships with others.

I also write and speak about *faith in yourself*, a strong ally in mastering your way to the top. This is faith in your objectives and goals as being honest and good and worthy of your best efforts. It's also faith in others. And above all, it is faith in the future. Faith can be a positive factor in your life, and therefore a positive factor in your business and all other actions you undertake to get to the top—and, more important, to stay there.

Consider the effect of faith on me—the faith of my mother, who all her life exercised the power of positive thinking. Norman Vincent Peale would have considered her a first-class example of the things he wrote about in his book *The Power of Positive Thinking*. I can still hear my mother saying, "Joey, I have faith in you, faith that you'll succeed in whatever field you choose. But you must have that same faith in *yourself*."

My mother handed down her faith in me, and I have been guided by it all my life. In turn, I have tried to give that faith to others. A familiar saying is that "The more you give something to others, the more you wind up having for yourself." Try it as you seek the faith you'll need to succeed.

So many things have been said or written about faith. You're probably familiar with many of them. For example, faith is said to move mountains. We all know that doesn't mean the Rockies or the Alps. But faith *can* move the mountains of self-doubt, frustration, discouragement, and negative thinking that get in your way toward success. Faith is said to be the assurance of things hoped for. I like to put a Girard spin on that. I believe that hoping will never get you anywhere, nor will wishing or expecting. You might say, "I sure hope it doesn't rain today." That's a nice thought, but your hope won't affect the weather at all. It will either rain or it won't rain, and your hoping has nothing to do with it. Wishing won't put you within a country mile of your goals. Instead, I believe that faith is the assurance of things or goals that are *planned for*, are *realistic*, and that call for *working smart*. Hoping won't change the weather, but *planning* for either bad weather or good weather will assure you are prepared for whatever weather comes. Put your faith in planning, not wishing. Only that kind of faith will get you to the top.

Faith in Humanity

At a panel discussion of business administration, a seminar student asked what the hardest business is to operate on a day-to-day basis. The answers ranged far and wide.

"A restaurant or cafe, small or large," one panel member suggested, "because the owner or chef can never be sure of how much food and what kind will be ordered by the diners each day. What will go like hotcakes one day will die in the kitchen the next. Unless the restaurant offers nothing but pizza, for instance, or furnishes a very limited menu, the owner is, each day, at the mercy of different appetites."

"A grocery store," another panel member said, "whether it's a mom-and-pop operation or a supermarket, because the profit margin is small, you face spoilage of fresh produce that isn't bought, and there's a great deal of employee stealing or customer shoplifting."

"I'd vote for one or more independent service stations," a third panel member cut in, "because of never-ending gasoline price wars and the uncertainty of what Middle East oil countries will do to the market. Late-night robbery is a big hazard, too."

A fourth panel member was silent for a moment, then said, "A hospital. Running a hospital, especially a small one, or even a large clinic is a risky business. Skilled doctors may or may not be skilled businessmen, and a hospital is a crisis-by-crisis operation. An emergency is the rule rather than the exception."

I was inclined to agree with that last opinion. When a hospital is mentioned, I usually think of the Mayo Clinic, but this time my mind went to something else. I think a hospital—whether one of few beds in a small community or as large as the Mayo Clinic—is certainly a business in every sense of the word. It better generate a profit or it will go under. In most countries hospitals operate in a straitjacket of government regulations, just as manufacturers do. The hours are long; the stress is great.

Nowhere could the stress have been greater than at the little hospital that Dr. Albert Schweitzer founded in Africa. That hospital flourished, and still does, because of Schweitzer's unshakable faith in others, an overwhelming faith in mankind, and, of course, a strong faith in himself.

I've written about a number of business success stories and about many successful individuals who began with nothing but a dream. Although some were dirt-poor, they had a spark that never went out. But most of them had more than a spark to light their fires. They had faith. They believed in miracles.

This book and my others are the result of a miracle.

The Miracle Lowell Thomas Started

If you were to drive down the eastern end of Detroit's Grand Boulevard, you'd see a big sign on a building that for years housed people who worked hand-in-hand with the folks at General Motors. It reads: "Faith Through Miracles." Fine. Except that, once again, I like to put a spin on that sign. When I read it, I change it to say: "Miracles Through Faith."

I've mentioned often how faith, when exercised, carried me through the early disappointments in my life. It sustained me when I was down, so broke that I hardly knew where to turn, and it rewarded me when I took the steps that carried me to the top. As faith worked, and still works, for me, so it can work for you.

I've mentioned Lowell Thomas before—and I will again. It was Lowell Thomas's faith in me that brought about a change in my career. Certainly Lowell Thomas needs no introduction. For years he was a network newscaster whose broadcasts were heard coast to coast. He was an adventurer and explorer, a writer, and an innovator. It was Lowell Thomas who first introduced the sensational screen presentation *This Is Cinerama*, the three-screen process that held viewers spellbound as they roared down a roller-coaster at dizzying speed or went with the camera into Notre Dame Cathedral in Paris. It was Lowell Thomas who gave a first-hand account of T. E. Lawrence, in his book *With Lawrence in Arabia*. This is one of the first times people learned about Lawrence, the English soldier and member of British Intelligence whose astonishing military achievements in the Middle East during World War I mystified the world.

What a career Lowell Thomas had. You can imagine how I felt when Thomas said to me, after hearing me speak, "Joe, you must write a book."

"I don't think I can," I said.

"Joe, I have faith in you." There was that word *faith* again. He introduced me to people in book publishing, and that miracle of human nature happened: He gave me faith in *myself*. He paved the way, and I went on to write books and later to give lectures all over the world. The memory of him lingers on, as does his cheery sign-off on his broadcasts, "So long until tomorrow."

For me, Lowell Thomas caused a miracle to happen. Not everyone may be as fortunate as I was in having a Lowell Thomas express his faith in me. Let me do for you what Lowell Thomas did for me. Let me tell you that I have faith in you. If I didn't, I could never say to you, as I do, that *you are number one!*

Faith Brings Fulfillment

You know that it was faith in his mission that kept Christopher Columbus pressing on in spite of perils at sea. That it was faith in the goal of freedom as a just cause that helped George Washington endure the cold and hunger at Valley Forge. That it was faith in the spirit of his people that gave strength to Winston Churchill during the darkest days of World War II. That it was faith that helped men like Richard DeVos, Jack LaLanne, Dale Carnegie, and Don Tocco. And it was faith that helped Muriel Siebert, Kaye Britton, and Judith Briles achieve their success. A lot of other elements helped them and others master their way to the top, but *faith* was right there, spurring them on.

Three Important Questions

As much as I've put my faith in faith, I've learned that it can knock the wind out of your sails and set you on course to another top—one just as important as the heights you're going for in the business or professional world. There is a very successful businessman who'll look you straight in the eye and tell you, "My cup runneth over." He's not talking necessarily about money. He's talking about the results that came from asking himself three questions. His name is Michael Timmis.

"I had the best of all possible worlds," he'll tell you. "I've had everything materially, yet I felt I had nothing. I felt totally unfulfilled." Timmis is vice chairman of the Talon Group, a billion-dollar umbrella corporation that comprises a sizable number of operations and lines of products: manufacturing; automotive, metal, and foam products; flexible packaging; sophisticated automated lines for the agricultural industry; a construction company; real estate development; and many others. It employs well over 6,000 workers—men, women, young people, minorities, handicapped—who are respected and happy because of the good business and management policies that Timmis and his partner follow.

Timmis is also vice chairman of F&M, named after Fred and Marge Cohen, its founders. Timmis and his partner bought F & M when it was just one store, and expanded it to over a hundred deep-discount drugstores located around the United States. It is one of the three largest such chains in the country. "A company of the nineties, in fact of the next century," Timmis declares.

"I couldn't have achieved business success without my partner," Timmis states. His long-standing partner is Randy Agley, a former accountant. "We dreamed together, worked together, and built Talon together through mergers and acquisitions. And I've loved what we built." *Build* is a word that Timmis uses often.

It wasn't a lack of fulfillment in terms of reaching the top from a climb up from nothing, or in terms of gaining wealth. He realized the lack as he examined his responses to questions that he put to himself from time to time. "I believe that everyone asks themselves at one time or another—or in one way or another—these three questions: Why am I here? What am I supposed to be doing? Where am I going? When you boil everything away, the answers are the real issues one must face."

For the first question, "Why am I here?" Timmis learned that it took time to find the real answer. "Being here" began when he was born, the youngest of five children of Irish-Canadian parents who believed that education was everything. They instilled in their kids a strong sense of self-worth and, above all, solid religious faith. "They made me understand," he said, "that as a child of God I was here to be part of the answers to the problems of the world around me, to enjoy the world and to give back to others what had been given to me." That faith, plus faith in himself, often sustained Michael Timmis in times of crisis. "All my life I've had faith in myself," he states.

The family was of modest means. His parents did not have a lot to give their children economically. After all, it was a family of seven. His mother was a 4'11" bundle of spunk who was everything one thinks of when "family values" are mentioned. His dad was a big, tough guy—a former football player with a set of powerful muscles, who worked for Detroit's Department of Street Railways back in the days when the city still had streetcars. Now and then a streetcar jumped the tracks. Timmis's dad took a steel bar, slipped it under the car, and bringing his unusual strength to bear, lifted it by himself right back onto the rails. He could lift the rear end of an automobile out of a ditch. His dad lived to be ninety-one.

Timmis's mother died when Michael was fifteen, and her death was a devastating blow. "I was very close to my mother. It was a tough period in my life. It made me tough." That was important because at the time he was a sickly lad, unable to take part in athletics with the other boys at school.

"I started to read," Timmis recalls, "and it changed my life. I became a voracious reader. It opened up the world to me." That plus his parents' strong faith in the importance of education helped him set his sights on college. It's no wonder that Timmis says, simply, "My mother and father were the most influential people in my life. They made me understand exactly why I was here."

The second question Timmis asked himself, "What am I supposed to be doing?" drew him to the law. College and law school were a long, hard row to hoe. He worked hard to make a buck. "I did every kind of job you can think of. I scrubbed and hand-cleaned labs, I was a scaffold painter, I worked nights at a pharmacy, I drove a car for a blind person, and I tutored other students." He not only earned his education but he also *learned* from the experience. "I learned to appreciate the hard efforts of working people. I became aware of the needs and sufferings that beset others."

Michael Timmis views law as a building block of society, not as a representative of an adversarial system. "Law should be used as a constructive force, not as a destructive or negative force." Timmis makes a comparison to the oft-quoted "Power tends to corrupt and absolute power corrupts absolutely." He believes that "negativism corrupts" and leads to dwelling on the downside of life. That's not where Timmis lives.

As he and his partner built their umbrella corporation, Timmis faced what often seemed insurmountable obstacles while putting in unbelievably long hours and making personal sacrifices. But his faith in himself and the free enterprise system remained unshaken. He recently received the prestigious Legend Award from Students in Free Enterprise for his accomplishments, and for his question-and-answer sessions with college students concerning the free enterprise system and the strong spiritual faith that maintains him. "I had self-doubts along the way to the top—what person hasn't?—but all my adult life I had faith that I could overcome obstacles." In overcoming those obstacles he was not alone. His wife stood beside him. "Day by day, my wife was and is my strength." Never was his faith more sorely tested nor the strength of his wife more needed, than when his fifteen-year-old daughter died.

"I always felt I had to be doing something, to achieve something." And he did. Through perseverence, hard work, good business ethics, and faith, his Talon Group grew and prospered. He gained prestige, influence, and wealth on his way to the top.

Despite prestige and wealth, Timmis felt unfulfilled. He found an answer to the third question, "Where am I going?" He took the time to be by himself, to be quiet, to reflect on his priorities. He came to this conclusion: The men and women who are true successes are those who realize that, in the big picture, their awareness and concern for the world around them are of greater importance than the power they may have gained in the business world.

Timmis began a journey of self-fulfillment by making faith in God his number one priority, the end of which was his emergence, he believes, as a complete, freer, and stronger person. "I realized," he says, "that I should be concerned about the world and not just myself. Fulfillment would come by contributing my time, talents, and resources to the world around me." Those who are trying to master their way to the top would do well to remember that prestige and wealth in and of themselves are nothing without a sense of self-fulfillment.

Timmis believes firmly that most of the world's problems, most of the inner-city problems, are due to alienation between peoples. He believes that problems resulting from racial and cultural differences, from a multitude of differing faiths, from poverty, hunger, disease, neglect, and a breakdown in family values, can be helped by reconciliation efforts.

Toward that goal, Michael Timmis declares, "We need unity, not division, among people. Men and women, working together for a common cause, can accomplish much. It's people who have the solutions to our problems. It doesn't take many people to build a critical mass to make change. I want to be an agent of reconciliation." He believes that being such an agent can move mountains. Remember, faith *can* move mountains. The Girard challenge is "Go ahead, move those mountains!"

AFANA

I frequently use the letters ATANA, meaning *All Talk And No Action*. Now add to that the letters AFANA, meaning *All Faith And No Action*. Faith without action counts for little. The Good Book says that faith without works is dead, and it means what it says. If you have faith in yourself, faith that you can be what you want to be, then *do* something about it.

I like the story about the farm country suffering from drought. It hadn't rained for months. The land was parched; the topsoil was blowing away; the crops were dying; the livestock was suffering. The minister of the little church in that area said one Sunday, "Let's all pray for rain this week. Exercise your faith and next Sunday let's look for a miracle—a cloudburst." Well, the dry spell continued all week. The following Sunday the minister asked the congregation, "Did you pray for rain?" All the people said aloud that they did. "Did you have faith that it would rain?" They all said, "Oh, yes, of course, yes." The minister smiled. "I don't believe you," he said. "If you had faith, you would have brought your umbrellas." No umbrellas. It was all faith and no action.

And speaking of rain, no one took action better than old Noah and his family. It's worth noting, as someone once said, that it wasn't raining when Noah *started* to build the ark.

17
Be Ambitious, Be Tough

HAVING THE AMBITION to master your way to the top is extremely important if you wish to achieve success. Whether it's in business or other endeavors, ambition is a driving force. I like to call it the spark that gets the engine going.

If your ambition is to pay off, you've got to be tough on yourself. If your ambition is to mean anything at all, you've got to be a master at practicing willpower. The trouble with many people is that they practice "won't power" instead of willpower. "Won't power" is like stabbing ambition in the back. I'm going to show you how to take "won't power" and turn it around to your advantage.

At one time in my life, I was guilty of almost letting "won't power" take over my life. It was because my dad constantly used the word *won't:* "You *won't* amount to anything, Joey." "You *won't* make it." "You *won't* get anywhere in life." I had to grit my teeth and counter with "I *will*, I *will*, I *will*." *I will* became the spark of my ambition.

Along the way, I wondered why so many people fail to exercise willpower during a real crunch. I'm sure psychologists could tick off any number of reasons. I'm no psychologist, but my personal belief is that using willpower is, for many, simply too much effort. Well, of course it calls for effort. It calls for being *tough*.

Think of the people you know (maybe even yourself) who have tried to quit smoking. They'll say, "Oh, I *can* quit smoking. No problem. I've quit lots of times." Then they keep right on puffing away. Even with all the warnings on the pack of cigarettes and the warnings in the ads, they keep right on. When I was a kid growing up in the Detroit ghetto, cigarettes were called coffin nails, but that didn't stop kids from smoking them. But I believe that exercising willpower, at any age, will overcome an addiction to nicotine. Also to alcohol. You must have the ambition to quit.

Here's another example. How many people do you know (maybe even yourself) who go on diets and then go off them in short order? They balloon up and deflate and then balloon up again. I was a good example of that. It took willpower to stick to a diet and to an exercise program. Ambition to take off the flab became my spark. Being tough on myself kept the spark alive.

I mastered my way to the top by learning to use "won't power" in a positive instead of a negative way. I simply used the *opposite* of willpower to good advantage and made it work for me. Be ambitious! Be tough! Use those words as you practice this Girard technique to develop the self-discipline necessary for willpower to really work for you.

I start each day with affirmations like these:

- I *won't* give up as I take the stairs to the top, one step at a time.
- I *won't* let obstacles get in my way. I'll kick them out of my path.
- I *won't* let others discourage me.
- I *won't* put off until tomorrow those things that I should do today.

- I *won't* quit anything I've started that's right for
  me to do.

By using "won't power" this way, something strange and wonderful takes place. You'll soon find yourself using willpower instead, and you'll be surprised at the results. You *will* push yourself to work smart. You *will* find yourself using your time to best advantage. You *will* be exercising self-discipline day after day. You *will* stay ambitious. You *will* be tough on yourself.

The Spark of Ambition

Whenever someone mentions "Big Boy" to me, I get an instant image of a chubby little fellow wearing checkered overalls, who is the symbol of the famous Big Boy double-decker hamburger. I suspect that image is true for just about everybody in this country. What you or I may not think of is the giant corporation known as Big Boy International. And perhaps you're not familiar with the success story of the Elias brothers—Fred, Louis, and John—who, starting with nothing but borrowed money and ambition, built Big Boy into one of the largest family-owned restaurant chains in the world. It's a system with sales of approximately $1 billion annually.

The Elias brothers, the sons of immigrants John and Jenny Elias, who came to America from Lebanon, inherited a strong belief in the American Dream, the value of hard work, and the certainty that they could achieve whatever they desired as long as the family stuck together.

The Elias brothers were like the Three Musketeers, whose slogan was "All for one and one for all." Fred, Louis, and John followed that philosophy. As they mastered their way to the top, no major decision was ever made unless all three agreed. The three brothers worked as one. "I know it's hard to believe that all three of us had to agree on every major decision," Fred Elias has often stated, "but that's the way we've run our business."

The Elias family first put down roots in Massachusetts, where the three brothers and two of their sisters were born. Fred, the oldest of the brothers, was followed by Louis and then John. In the early 1930s, the family moved to Detroit, Michigan, where the third sister was born. Mother and father and the three brothers and three sisters were very poor. In the midst of the Great Depression, Fred had to quit school and work to help support the family.

His uncle, who owned a bakery, gave him a job delivering baked goods to local restaurants. He worked long hours, seven days a week. In time his brothers joined him. They believed strongly in the work ethic. And ambition surely was a spark for the Elias brothers as they forged ahead. From their father they gained the traits of absolute honesty and fairness in all their dealings. Their father also taught them that through hard work and ambition they could control their own destiny. That destiny was to own their own business.

Again, I like to think of working hard as working smart, and that's what underscored all their efforts—working smart to achieve their ambition. Add to that, enthusiasm. In 1937, Fred got a job as manager of a restaurant. The restaurant business excited him very much, and the excitement was contagious. Louis and John caught the fever, along with their older brother, of "starting out on their own." Thus, control of their destiny began in 1938, when the three brothers opened a small restaurant that they called, in honor of the eldest brother, Fred's Chili Bowl. Talk about a humble start. Their first day of business they took in $17.

Prior to and during World War II, the two younger brothers saw military service. Louis joined the navy and John the navy air force. Louis returned home in 1941 and helped Fred at the Chili Bowl. And the little restaurant prospered. Enthusiasm for the restaurant business remained in high gear. Using the family furniture as collateral, Fred and Louis borrowed money to open a small diner, which they called the Dixie Drive-In. They served hand-ground, pure-beef hamburgers. As always, and rooted in Old World tradition, every member of the Elias family chipped in. Mother cooked the Dixie Drive-In's popular chili, father made root beer, the sisters worked behind the counter, and Fred and Louis kept busy providing popular service.

In 1945, the war over, Young John returned to join his brothers. The Elias brothers opened a second restaurant, which they also called Dixie Drive-In. It became one of the first curbside restaurants in the Midwest. Again, it was a family affair. The Eliases cooked and scrubbed and delivered food to the cars. By 1952, there were four prospering Dixie Drive-Ins.

Along the way, however, their destiny took a dramatic change in direction. The year 1948 turned out to be a fateful one for the brothers. Unknown to them, in far-away Glendale, California, a fellow named Bob Wian had, from beginnings as humble as the Eliases, bought a small diner called Bob's Pantry. From Bob's Pantry emerged a new taste treat for hamburger-hungry folks. Wian had invented the first double-decker hamburger to tempt the taste buds—a meal in itself featuring a special sauce. A sketch of a young, chubby, curly-topped lad who swept out the diner became the symbol of the double-decker. At first Wian called it a Fat Boy, but he soon changed the name to Big Boy. Bob's Big Boy Restaurant chain began to grow.

In 1948, just about the time Fred, Louis, and John were about to open their third Dixie Drive-In, the three brothers attended the National Restaurant Association meeting in Chicago, Illinois. There they met Bob Wian, were charmed by him, and began a friendship that was to alter their destiny. The brothers learned that Wian operated with the same philosophy as they did: absolute cleanliness, quality food, and service second to none. They visited Wian's restaurant in California.

"Bob Wian was unlike any other restaurant man we knew," Fred states. "He really cared about his employees, his people enjoyed paid vacations, a pension plan and many other perks." Perhaps from his example, the Elias brothers enjoy a closeness with their employees. They care about them, keep in touch with them, respect them, and operate on a first-name basis. They never hold grudges.

Wian offered the three brothers the franchise rights for Big Boy in the city of Detroit. Once again the three reached a unanimous decision: not Detroit—all of Michigan. They got it. The Dixie Drive-Ins changed their names to Elias Brothers Big Boy Restaurants. The fifth in the chain had a greater seating capacity and offered a broader menu. Yet the popular Big Boy double-decker hamburger was the drawing card. The brothers knew they were heading for the top. They set their sights on having 100 restaurants by the mid-1960s. Ambition? By the mid-1970s, they had another hundred, some of them subfranchised. The sons of immigrants, the Elias boys were on their way to achieving the American Dream.

Most of the success stories in this book deal with individuals who have mastered their way to the top. But the principles apply equally to partners or teams. In many cases the old saying "Two heads are better" is true. Imagine, then, how a team of three can make it to the top.

"All for one and one for all!" The Elias brothers always went for the whole shooting match. For example, Marriott, the hotel people, had earlier bought out Bob Wian and were operating the Big Boy chain. When Marriott decided to get out of the restaurant business, the Elias brothers said "Let's get it!"

And get it, they did. They let nothing sideline them. They've followed the same principle I've followed in mastering my way to the top: Put blinders on and keep your eye steady on the finish line.

In 1987, Elias Brothers restaurants acquired the worldwide franchise rights for the international Big Boy System, the tenth largest privately held family-restaurant business, with well over 1,000 restaurants in the United States, Canada, Japan, and Saudi Arabia, and with over 17,000 employees. There are over twenty franchisees worldwide, plus company-owned restaurants and concession operations at stadiums and arenas, commissaries, and warehouses. Louis Elias is chairman of the board; John and Fred are deceased.

From a $17 first day's earnings to an international structure, during which the Elias brothers found time along the way for athletics, many private philanthropies, community involvement, and charities support. Low key and modest, they lived a simple life. The Big Boy restaurants were one of the first to offer menus in Braille. But you don't need to read Braille to know that the Elias brothers, with their dedication to hard work, their steadfast ambition, and their family unity, provide inspiration to all who want to master their way to the top.

Old-Fashioned Virtues

There is a lot to be learned from the Elias brothers about ambition and about working together to reach a common goal. (Joe and Barbara Scaglione, whom I wrote about in Chapter 6, are another fine example of two people working together to succeed.) The Elias brothers were self-disciplined. Whenever the going got rough, they were tough enough to face the obstacles and overcome them. They had a strong will to win.

The American Dream was more than a dream to them; they believed it to be a reality, and they set out to make it so. They also knew that to turn a dream into reality required working smart, and doing so regardless of the time it took or the wait before they could roll down their sleeves and call it a day.

I certainly don't believe that an Old World background is responsible, even in part, for the successes enjoyed by so many people I've known or met. There are too many successes by

Americans generations removed from ancestors who emigrated to the New World. The work ethic is not the sole property of immigrants, but the fact remains that many of the qualities needed to master your way to the top derive from the so-called old-fashioned virtues of ambition, hard work, and toughness brought to this country from distant shores.

18
Battle to Excel

TOM MONAGHAN IS a battler. Talking with him, I thought perhaps I should call this chapter "How to Battle Your Way to the Top." Tom states: "To me, the real substance of life and work is a constant battle to excel."

When we discussed his early life, I was struck by how similar our boyhoods and early youth were. He certainly knew what it was like to be dirt-poor; so did I.

He knew what it was like to be rejected, often by those he loved most; so did I. He sold newspapers as a kid; so did I. He set pins in bowling alleys; so did I. He loved and still loves cars with a passion; so do I.

Even as a preteen he sought work in a car dealership, asking for no pay, but just the chance to be around automobiles. I went to work in a car dealership asking for nothing but a desk in an empty corner of a dealership's second floor, a telephone, and a directory.

He was a boxer, an athlete; I boxed too, in the Golden Gloves tournaments.

He was a tough, street-smart kid; so was I.

Tom keeps a sharp eye on his weight, and controls it

through calorie limits and exercise. I try to keep a sharp eye on my diet and the exercises taught me by Jack LaLanne.

We also share the same religious faith.

Tom Monaghan owns Domino's Pizza, with international headquarters at Domino's Farms in Ann Arbor, Michigan. Today, Domino's Pizza has over 5,600 stores with annual sales of over $2.5 billion. But what a battle it was for Tom to master his way to the top!

The Tossed Around Kid

Tom Monaghan was born in 1937. He was born into poverty. His father died when Tom was four years old, a traumatic shock to the young lad and an event that was to cause a major upheaval in his and his brother's life.

At that time his mother's earnings were slim and she had only a small amount from his dad's insurance. She used it to pay off the mortgage on their very small home. She wanted to return to school and become a registered nurse. But two small boys, especially such a lively, constantly curious one as Tom, were too much for her to cope with. She put Tom and his kid brother, Jim, in a series of foster homes. They were tossed around from one home to another, sometimes in one for only a few weeks.

Tom had a great talent for pranks and mischief, a talent that's not always appreciated by adults. While in the first grade, Tom was put into an orphanage with his brother. He loved the architecture of the converted, massive Victorian mansion, a love for architecture that he has carried all his life. But that was all he loved about the institution. "It was like a prison," he told me. "I wanted to get out, to not be there. I wanted to be like kids who had both parents and live a normal life."

He certainly didn't like the circumstances he was in, but

he knew at the time that he couldn't control his own destiny. Destiny at the orphanage meant a lot of discipline and hard work. Every kid there had chores assigned to him. Tom cut the grass, scrubbed and polished floors, ironed clothing, and cleaned the stair railings. "I figured that someday I'd grow up and I'd be everything I could be. I always seemed to have a lot of confidence in myself."

He got out of the orphanage when he was twelve years old, and he and his brother went to live with their mother in a resort city in the northwest corner of Michigan's lower peninsula. "It was the happiest day of my life. From a 'prison' to total freedom."

But not freedom from want. The family was still poor. "We lived in a very small, humble house," he states. "I didn't have many clothes. I began to notice things about poverty. I noticed what the other kids had, and I wanted the same things, too." So he worked a lot. "I went from door to door asking for jobs; I sold papers; I shoveled snow; I picked cherries; I sold fish that I caught in Lake Michigan; I was a soda jerk and a busboy; and did I set pins! I was a great pinsetter; in fact, I could set four lanes at a time."

Tom's boyhood work life reminds me a lot of my own. Tom didn't shine shoes, but I did. And I had a shoe-shine promotion that I know Tom, loving a good promotion as he does now, would have appreciated. I'd set my little shoebox in front of a man who needed a shine. "The shine is free," I'd say, and then I'd set to work and polish one shoe. Finished, I'd start to move on. "Wait a minute," the customer would say, "I thought the shine was free." I replied that it was. "I told you the truth, I just gave your shoe a free shine. To shine the other one costs a dime."

Even out of the orphanage, Monaghan's life was a long way from the multimillion-dollar pizza delivery empire he heads today. His battle to excel had just begun. "I don't know if it was from being poor," Monaghan says, "but I always wanted to have the best of everything. Or maybe it was because I was made fun of a lot when I was in school. I was wearing rags, I was small for my size. Some of the older kids picked on me. I felt I was different because I had been tossed around in foster homes and wound up in an orphanage.

"It started in those early days. I wanted to be the best in sports, to be the best dressed, and later to have the best cars. I made it a hobby back then to know what the best of just about everything was." Getting the best of everything had to wait a while. "I wanted to show them. They fueled my fire. I had to be number one—perhaps in later years, to a fault."

On into high school, he decided he wanted to study for the priesthood. "I wanted to be a priest ever since I was in the second grade," he declares. With help, he was accepted at a seminary in Michigan. "I studied hard to be a priest, but the discipline seemed on a par with life in the orphanage." In the tenth grade he was told that he didn't have a vocation. Despite his battle to excel at the seminary, his plea for another chance, he was asked to leave. He was very upset about it, and he finished high school elsewhere.

Semper Fi!

Monaghan didn't have enough money to go to college, so he joined the Marine Corps. He did a lot of guard duty and the corps moved him around a bit. He was a Marine for three years. The drill instructors—the DIs—were tough, and though Tom admits he was no saint, he didn't admire their language. He also admits the corps was good for him. While on a troop ship between the Philippines and Japan, he came up with a homemade philosophy for himself. It consisted of five personal priorities. "I thought it was the right format for a person's life—my life—and I haven't changed them since the day I developed them." As in the Marine Corps's motto, *Semper Fi*, he remains faithful to the five and here is how he sees them:

- *Spiritual.* "My religious faith is strong. Without it, I would never have been able to build Domino's. Whenever I've been floored by difficulties, my faith has helped me get back on my feet. That's the power of faith. I use it every day. In business matters, I express my faith by the Golden Rule: Do unto others as you would have them do unto you."
- *Social.* "First on my social scale of activities is my family, my wife and four daughters. Then come friends. You cannot succeed in business without friends. Next is community involvement. I believe that business has a responsibility to participate in community programs. The community supports you; you in turn support the community."
- *Mental.* "A clear conscience is what makes a healthy mind, one that has a positive, optimistic attitude and outlook. To remain healthy, the mind needs exercise. It should ask questions, be hungry for information, so that an individual can find answers to his own problems."
- *Physical.* "A healthy body is as important as a healthy mind. The body is the temple of the soul. I work out, I do pushups, I run. I take a physical exam every nine months. I've been called a fitness freak. I take that as a compliment."
- *Financial.* "I knew if I followed the first four priorities, financial success would follow. And it has. I put this one on the bottom where it belonged, but unfortunately I was often more interested in it than I was in the others. That's the one that can lead to mistakes. I made many."

The Beginning of Domino's

Monaghan's young life after the Marines was full of ups and downs, certainly in the financial area. He had saved money while in the corps, and then he invested it in the oil business. He invested more again and still more. He lost it all. The investment brought him nothing; the man to whom he turned over the money disappeared. Broke, he bummed around a bit. Once in Denver he spent the night in a mission in the slums. He spent nights in flophouses on skid row, and he'd pick up work setting pins again at bowling alleys.

It seemed that the battle to excel was harder than ever to wage. That is, until opportunity knocked at the door of a pizza store. He was twenty-three when he and his brother opened a small pizza shop at the edge of a university campus in southeastern Michigan. It was called DomiNick's, named after the man they bought it from. Tom and his brother borrowed $900 and used $500 as a down payment. Shortly after opening the store, Tom's brother bowed out. Tom originally thought he'd use the profits from the store to pay his way through college, but he soon found that he liked the pizza business. He liked making pizza, and before long he knew he was in the pizza business to stay and that he would make a success of it. He told himself, "If it's to be, it's up to me." The battle to excel began in earnest. His faith told him, "Assume, assume, assume it's going to happen."

At the beginning he did everything. He made the pizza, then closed the shop, delivered that pizza, then hurried back to make another. He couldn't make deliveries the first month because he didn't have a telephone. "I never had any doubts that I'd be successful. It just took hard work." You bet it did. Monaghan found himself working about a hundred hours a week, seven days a week other than holidays. He did this for thirteen years. "I had one vacation," he says, "six days when I got married.

"Margie's a great wife, I married an opposite. She's down to earth, level-headed, a great mother, a great sport. She's helped me to keep my feet on the ground. We lived in a house trailer when we were first married. She kept all the books for the company for a number of years, and paid the bills. She was there when I came home every night." He smiles. "I'm the kite and she's the string."

Of course, there were setbacks. The original owner of the pizza shop had allowed Monaghan to use his name, DomiNick's. After a while he said he wanted Tom to stop using it. With a lot of thought and some sudden inspiration, the name was changed to Domino's.

But there is also sugar sold under the brand name of Domino, and efforts were made by that company to prevent Monaghan from using the name. After lawsuits and appeals, Monaghan won the right to keep the name Domino's Pizza.

And there was a time when he was hopelessly insolvent. He challenged himself to get out of debt no matter how long it took. "From 1969 to 1973, I just took things day by day," he says, "and I figured some day, somehow, I'd pay everybody off until I was out of debt."

He says he always seemed to be in and out of trouble, but each time, luckily, he'd come back stronger if not necessarily wiser. But I don't believe luck had anything to do with it. He came back stronger because he fought the good fight. Monaghan has always been strongly competitive, but he also believes that success in business is hollow unless you master your way to the top honestly and fairly, by playing strictly by the rules. He is an idealist (there should be more like him), and he is deeply committed to his business, to his employees, to his customers, to his faith, and to the moral principles that guide his activities.

As the first Domino's Pizza multiplied into several stores, he multiplied them even more by franchising. Monaghan built his business as an architect might, from a design that was a mental picture. He is an architect of ideas and patterns, a disciple of Frank Lloyd Wright. Indeed, Monaghan is certain that Wright was the greatest architect in the world. Domino's international headquarters reflects Wright's style, with a long and low building that blends with the terrain.

The Best of Everything

With success came an increased urge to have the best of everything. "I was always willing to wait longer and work harder and dream bigger than other people seemed to. But I tended to go whole hog in everything I got interested in and I sometimes overdo it." For example, Monaghan points out that he thinks he spent more money in a couple of years than anybody else in the country. "I bought a World Series–winning major league baseball team; I developed the Domino's Farm complex of buildings, picnic areas, museum for my antique cars, and farm-animal petting area; and I built a lodge on Drummond Island in Lake Huron. I bought private jet airplanes, a helicopter, a yacht, and more cars. I justified it all at the time."

Tom Monaghan has a different perspective now. "I'm cured of having to do that sort of thing. I'm not going to do it for the rest of my life. I'm not going to buy anything to impress anybody. I've got it out of my system." So, in addition to material things, what has the battle to excel won for Monaghan in terms of spiritual priorities? He finds that simple things—enduring family values and a desire to spread his faith by being a living example of it—are the things that count. They are the things that money can't buy. This is evidenced by his work with Legatus, an organization he founded. Legatus is an international organization composed of Catholic CEOs committed to study, spread and apply their faith in their professional and personal lives. "I believe there is something bigger in life, and more important, than Domino's. I have faith that I will find it."

That search, I believe, will bring Tom Monaghan strength and endurance. That "something bigger in life than Domino's" may be his greatest success of all. Now it's your turn to join the battle to excel. Courage!

19
Six Simple Steps to Success

A<small>T ONE TIME</small> or another you've probably found yourself halted at a railroad crossing while a seemingly endless chain of freight cars passed by, or backed up and then went forward again. You wondered when the warning lights would stop flashing, the bell would quit ringing, and the gate would lift.

You could sit at the wheel of your car and fume, or you could tell yourself, as I've learned to do, to be patient. Patience can be a key to success—not the only key, but one key. I thought about that recently as I waited at a railroad crossing. And I thought about a friend for whom trains were and still are a passion.

As a three-year-old in Ohio, Richard Kughn used to love watching trains go by at railroad crossings. He'll tell you, with a nostalgic look in his eyes, "When I was little I could stand there by the hour just watching." Track stretching beyond his world at the time, cars both freight and passenger, fascinated him.

"I was walking home from school," he told me. "It was garbage pick-up day. There was a trash barrel with a Lionel train set sticking out of the top." He pulled the set out—the train, the track, the transformer—took it home, and cleaned it up. "We had a Ping-Pong table in the basement, and my dad helped me set the track on it. The darn thing worked." That, at seven, was his first train. Two years later he received a new set for Christmas—a locomotive, box and tank cars, and a caboose on an oval track—and thus began a love affair with electric trains that has continued well over fifty years to this day.

When, as a boy, he was ill and quarantined for six weeks with scarlet fever, Kughn pored through every Lionel electric-train catalog that he could put his hands on. He dreamed that if only he owned the company that made them, he could have his pick of any one, or all, of them. An impossible dream? Not at all. Today he owns Lionel Trains, Inc.

Richard Kughn is DBA (Doing Business As) Kughn Enterprises, not only for Lionel Trains but nearly a score of other business organizations including Longbow Productions, a highly successful motion picture production company, and the prestigious Whitney Restaurant in Detroit. Kughn restored a historic, century-old mansion and turned it into a three-story showplace of polished oak and mahogany, gleaming chandeliers, tuxedo-wearing waiters, fine linen and table settings, and, above all, a menu that is to food what a Rolls-Royce is to automobiles. Sitting across from Kughn, one can't fail to catch his enthusiasm, sense his driving spirit, and marvel at his love of life and people. "Call me Dick" is the immediate way he puts people at ease.

Born in Detroit and raised in Ohio, Dick is today worth many millions and is an awesome business success as both a real estate developer and an industrialist. He is a member of nearly forty boards, some of which are business memberships, some academic affiliations, and some civic organizations. He has chaired some of those boards and has shared his strengths and business know-how in other capacities. He is a man of many hobbies, is active in over a dozen social clubs, and has been awarded honors ranging from induction into his high school Distinguished Alumni Hall of Fame to being appointed by Michigan's governor as Ambassador of Michigan Tourism, from Michiganian of the Year to Humanitarian of the Year, and many more.

Kughn's success and affluence came only after traveling a road that was filled with setbacks and frustration. The fact that he mastered his way to the top despite setbacks makes his success story all the more remarkable. His life is bound to be an inspiration to young men and women just starting their careers, with their sights aimed at the top.

A Positive Family Background

Many of the success stories in this book are of people who overcame poverty, who came from extremely humble beginnings. Such is not the case with Dick Kughn. He was born into a middle-class family.

"Actually, a little lower than middle class," as he puts it. "I was fed and clothed well, but as far as a lot of extras, nope. There were not a lot of frills. My dad, actually my stepfather who had adopted me and who was a real estate title examiner, was a good provider. I had a great mother and father. They were a great influence on my life. They created a sense of pride in me, a sense of pride in accomplishment that started when I was a little boy."

Dick, like others I've known and written about, credits his parents for their encouragement to succeed. They not only provided encouragement and support in his efforts but supported him when he was frustrated by what he calls his vision problem. He told me that vision was one hardship that he had to endure. "I was born with eyes that didn't 'work together.' They still don't." Dick told me that the condition is called vertical diplopia, something which gives him double vision. As a teenager and again as an adult, he had several operations, with some success. He remembers that when he was fifteen or sixteen, eye surgeons told his mother that there was nothing they could do about his eyes.

"I couldn't read even for five minutes. I'd see two different lines. Consequently I was an extremely poor high school student. The school counselor told me that although tests showed I ranked very high among all engineering students at a university level, and very high in political sciences, there was no way I could get into a university because of my academic record."

Let me tell you, the Joe Girard academic record wasn't so hot either, and I had good eyes. Dick Kughn asked the same question that I had: "What should I do with my life?" To locate an answer to that question, he rolled up his sleeves and went to work.

Love of a Challenge

Although he came from a comfortable home, Dick was no stranger to work. This future multimillionaire sold the *Saturday Evening Post* and the *Ladies' Home Journal*. He peddled newspapers and a "Shopping News." While still in high school, he was a theater usher. He convinced the manager to let him put on nearly hour-long magic shows (he had also fallen in love with magic), during which, with student assistants, he performed feats of levitation and other illusions. When he got his driver's license, he started his own lawn service.

Out of high school, Dick knew he would have to do things that didn't depend entirely on use of his eyes. Never once, reflecting upon his vision problems, did he sing the sad song, "Poor me, why me?" To him, whatever he did was a challenge, and all his life he has loved a challenge.

Dick Kughn told me of a sports challenge he faced when in high school. Although the football season had started, he decided to go out for the football team. "I was a skinny kid, weighing 147 pounds," he grinned, "and I was told I was too light and that I also was too late. But I persevered. I wound up on the team, playing a 147-pound right tackle, the lightest guy in the league playing on the line."

He worked for a year selling vacuum cleaners door to door, and he admits that was really tough selling. In Detroit, he worked for a while at an automobile body manufacturing company as an inspector. Then, in Baltimore, he became a timekeeper on a construction job and he fell in love with construction. I can relate to that, for I had once been a builder.

But always on his mind was that he wanted more than ever to go to Ohio University and study engineering. He went back to his high school counselor who, offering encouragement, made it possible for Dick to take an entrance exam that he passed with flying colors. "I had the ability," he told me, "but my eyes were, once more, the big problem. I was really trying to study, but my eyes got in the way." Dick got through the first semester, then his eye doctor got him excused from school to undergo surgery again, with the possibility he could resume later on. He returned to Detroit, had eye surgery, then went to work on a construction job, a government housing project. Talk about challenges. He started off as a laborer on a concrete gang, then worked with carpenters on forms, then as labor foreman, then as a materials inspector.

"When the Field Project Engineer left, the company, knowing I was planning to go back to school, told me that they'd like me to stay on and finish the project. It would take another fourteen months, which would mean I'd miss a year of school. If you want the job, it's yours." That called for thought, another key to success, but not *the* key. He gave it a lot of thought; totaling up the pros and cons, he took the job. He was transferred to Chicago to work on a veterans hospital job. He was on his way up in the construction business, working in Illinois, Michigan, and Ohio. In Cleveland, he became a cost engineer and, a little later, had the chance to become an estimator. He was on the mark when it came to estimating materials and costs.

He persevered. Perseverance was another key to success, but alone, it was not *the* key. I'm sure you're beginning to see a pattern. Some people may call them six secrets for success but, as you know, I believe you get to the top by taking the right steps along the way.

Six Simple Steps to Success

As a student, Dick Kughn set out to prove that there were three steps in life that could help him overcome any obstacle. They were the moral of a little story he had written based on Brer Rabbit and the Briar Patch. They were:

1. *Patience.* All things come to those who wait. Often opportunities come by default.
2. *Thought.* Think it over. Consider all angles. Don't aim headlong in whatever direction the wind is going.
3. *Perseverance.* Hang in there. Keep your eyes on your goals. Don't give up on your dreams.

As he forged ahead, Kughn found that those three steps were not enough to overcome obstacles, so he added three more:

4. *Need for people.* You can't go it alone when traveling the road to success. People supply support.
5. *Teamwork.* If you're going to have people around you, if you're going to involve others, you must have teamwork and the communication that goes with it.
6. *Networking.* As your relationships with people keep expanding, you need to develop a network.

If you leave a good impression and treat people
properly, you'll have a network of contacts who
come back to you without even calling upon them.

These principles have served Dick Kughn well. His background in costing and estimating led to an opportunity to work with a gentleman who was destined to become one of the major developers and builders of shopping centers and malls in the nation. That gentleman was Al Taubman. Dick began as an estimator for Taubman, later bought into the company, worked his way up to become its president and chief operating officer, and, finally, to vice chairman of the board.

But Dick hankered to be on his own, so he left the Taubman organization. It was then that he bought the Whitney mansion that I mentioned earlier and formed Kughn Enterprises. While moving steadily forward in his quest to get ahead in the world, he never put aside his love for model trains. In his late twenties he started collecting toy trains, and he became active in model train clubs.

Mr. Lionel

Dick is called Mr. Lionel. In the mid-1980s he heard that the Lionel Train Company was for sale. The manufacture of model trains had been moved from Michigan to Mexico, where operations, both in workmanship and marketing, frankly were a disaster. "I wanted to move everything back to Michigan where the Lionel Company started and where I felt it belonged. I wanted to continue the tradition." It was a dream born in those days when he had scarlet fever. But as I've pointed out in an earlier chapter, he *dared to dream*. Dreams can come true.

Dick was determined to buy the operation and, although he was advised by financial experts not to do so, he went ahead. He had been patient through the years, he gave the matter much thought, and he persevered until Lionel was back in Michigan. He knew he would have to develop a team of good people. Today the decades-old company is flourishing; it surpassed $50 million a year in just two years after he bought it.

Model railroads are laid out in Dick's private museum (soon to be a conference center) with thousands of feet of track, complete with landscaping, stations and other buildings, switches, and signals. Want to see the locomotives and cars roll? "Just say Lionel," Dick told me, and he obliges. And rolling stock that isn't set up on great replicas of terrain rests on multiple shelves that line the walls.

Along with his love of trains is Dick's love of cars. Starting at the age of two, he played with toy cars: "I'd lay out playing cards on the floor and pretend they were roads. I had a great love for automobiles as I grew up, just a natural love." Once, walking home from school with a friend, Dick said, "Let's build a car." So they built one out of junkyard parts. It was a 1923 Model T touring car. "I drove it all through my senior year in high school. That's what really got me turned on to automobiles."

I had that love for cars, too, and I loved to sell them— so much so that my sales record put me in the *Guinness Book of Records*. But Dick has set a different kind of automobile record. He turned his love for automobiles into acquiring the finest. His impressive collection of automobiles from the 1920s and earlier, through the 1950s, 1960s, and 1970s, many in the same private museum as his model trains, ranks among the ten best collections in the country and is the envy of car buffs everywhere.

From a kid who sold the *Saturday Evening Post* to an industrialist worth millions, Dick Kughn remembers that his pockets weren't always lined with silver. A man of accomplishment, yes, but he's also a man of humility. He recalls his early struggles. At age twenty and out of a job, he was heading back from Chicago to Detroit: "I had only twelve bucks in my pocket, and I was driving an old coupé, with all my worldly possessions, which weren't much. On the way, I had a blowout that ruined the tire. On top of that, I was almost out of gas. I got to a nearby station. Together, a retread and gas at that time cost me eight dollars. With only four bucks left, I bought bread and jam and a jar of peanut butter for dinner, and took a room at a Detroit YMCA."

Here's a man who, although he had double vision that couldn't be helped by surgery, always kept his eyes on the road ahead, whether it was playing cards stretched out on the floor or railroad tracks reaching into the distance, or simply the road to success.

But there's another factor that Dick Kughn didn't include in his six steps for reaching the top, although he mentioned it to me. It has to do with *liking* what you do, with satisfaction, with having fun while you're getting it done. "Along with doing the best you can at whatever you do, enjoy it," he states. "If I can't enjoy what I do, I'm going to get out of doing it."

I think that's a key to what makes not only a successful man but a happy one.

20
Failure Can Mean Success

I'M SURE YOU'RE familiar with the phrase "When one door closes, another one opens," or "Out of a bad experience, something good can come." I have a friend who can prove it. He's done so throughout his life.

We both have the same first name: Joe. He's billed by many as "The World's Number One Ad Copy Man," and that achievement alone should put him in the *Guinness Book of Records*. He's Joseph Sugarman, head of JS & A Group, Inc., Northbrook, Illinois, a north shore community near Chicago.

Joe is a man who used the power of the pen to build a major corporation that grosses well over $50 million annually. He didn't come from a rich family, and when he started he had no money. He did it all on his own; he's been doing it "on his own" all his life. How he mastered his way to the top is a story that will inspire young men and women today who are starting their careers with their feet on the ground and their eyes focused on the top.

Joe Sugarman grew up in Oak Park, Illinois, a city where the famed author Ernest Hemingway had lived and where the architect Frank Lloyd Wright had designed many homes and had been a teacher in Joe Sugarman's high school. It was a place steeped in tradition; one such tradition was that a young man went to college.

Joe did, although he never finished. His father was an entrepreneur, a promoter, and Joe was raised in an environment where one day there was money in the family and the next day his dad would be broke, where one day they lived in a fine home and the next day they were unable to pay the mortgage. Joe couldn't count on his family for financial support for his education, nor did he want to. While in college, he knew he had to get a job.

"I happened to be at a restaurant," he told me, "and the owner, seeing that I was a college student, mentioned that he'd like to get more students to come to his restaurant, but that he didn't know how. I suggested that he put an ad in the college paper and, without any writing experience at the time, I offered to compose it."

Joe wrote a really wild and crazy ad for the restaurant and almost immediately the place was deluged with students. The restaurant owner was overjoyed and offered a deal: If Joe kept writing ads for him, he'd give him all the food he could eat. Joe saw an opportunity. He began writing ads for a clothing store and for another restaurant, and soon he was steadily writing exciting ads in exchange for clothing and food. "I became the best-fed, best-dressed man on the campus," he recalls, a grin lighting up his bearded features. Thus began the career of the world's premier ad copy man.

Seated across from Joe Sugarman, listening to his enthusiastic approach to life and business, I quickly see that his words, voice, and smile let you know at once that Joe's a salesman first and foremost. He didn't have to tell me so. Being the World's Number One Retail Salesman myself proves that "It takes one to know one."

He's other things as well: a pilot, a sports fan, a lecturer, an author, and, in his younger days, an aspiring electrical engineer. Sugarman started a mail-order business for electronic products at the beginning of the 1970s. He conducted his operation in one room in his home at first, and in short order he needed nearly the entire house, including the basement. Between then and now he has known incredible success and equally incredible failure.

Success and failure in marketing products and services is one thing, but how Sugarman handled success and failure is, I believe, a far more important thing. It is a philosphy of coping that I recommend, but first let's look at the nature of Joe's business, because success in business is a main thrust in this book.

The JS & A Group, Inc.

The group is composed of a number of companies involved in marketing a wide variety of products—for example, BluBlocker sunglasses that shield the wearer's eyes by filtering out harmful ultraviolet rays, and that caused other sunglass manufacturers to rethink their product along the same lines; vitamin products; skin-care products; and automotive products such as windshield wipers and fuel conditioners.

Early in his career, Sugarman used direct marketing to introduce the first pocket calculators. He broadened the product line to include such items as rubbing oil for sore muscles, a personal blood-pressure computer, an automatic phone dialer, a pocket citizen-band radio, numerous health and fitness products, an ionized air purifier, a liquid crystal digital wristwatch, and numerous other products.

He sold directly to the consumer—in fact, Sugarman was the first to use toll-free telemarketing. He created ads that didn't look like ads; they resembled informative, often entertaining articles that appeared in newspapers and magazines such as airline in-flight publications. He also sold directly to the consumer through TV commercials, pointing out that the product could not be bought in retail outlets, only by writing for them or using a toll-free phone number. Major credit cards were welcome.

Though he is chairman of the companies in the JS & A Group, Inc., Sugarman really enjoys a unique status, one that the majority of successful business leaders cannot claim. "My role in the company," he told me one day over a pleasant get-together in Las Vegas, Nevada, "is basically creative. I'm a writer, and my skill is simply being able to write advertising copy that persuades people to purchase whatever product or service I have to offer." He not only writes persuasive ads for the print media, but also writes and produces his half-hour TV commercials, thus transferring his communicating skills to the video medium.

Joe states that one of the most rewarding business experiences for him is when he writes an ad or does a TV commercial, and people respond and buy his products. "To me, it's like the public is voting," he told me, "and saying 'yes, we like what you're offering, we're excited about it, and we're willing to exchange our hard-earned money for it.' Remember, money is really an extension of one's ego, and fortunately I can appeal to that ego."

Success and Failure

I asked Joe Sugarman about successes and failures in business as he mastered his way to the top. He said: "I've had a lot of failures throughout my life, and actually I'm very proud of them. Some of them were depressing, some quite sad, and some of them were funny."

I gathered that the latter were not funny ha-ha, but funny peculiar. How often have you heard that if you build a better mousetrap the world will beat a path to your door? It didn't quite work that way for Joe Sugarman. Consider a laser-beam mousetrap. It sounds like a winner in this laser-beam age. It certainly fit Joe's ongoing quest for unique products. "I spent thousands upon thousands of dollars in developing and promoting that mousetrap. It didn't make a single sale. So I dumped it."

That story illustrates Joe Sugarman's philosophy about success and failure: Rarely do you learn from success. "From all of my failures, however, I learned things. That's why I really cherish my failures. I'm convinced that failure is a learning process. I believe in certain forces, that there are success forces and that there are failure forces. One of the success forces, strange as it may seem, is failure itself.

"Every time you fail," he explains, "you are forced closer to success. Fail enough times and the knowledge gained puts you in a very strong position to achieve success. A lot of this has to do with belief. I've always felt—even when I lost everything I'd achieved, which I did on a couple of occasions—that I was still going to be a huge success, that it was just a matter of time."

Joe told me that he simply put failures into his back pocket, considering them experiences from which he learned much, and bounced back. Again and again he'd tell himself, "I know I'm going to make it!" It was that belief that kept him going. He is certain that belief in one's self can move mountains. "If people really believe they're going to be successful," he affirms, "they will be, despite failures."

Joe is living proof of this. He's been wiped out in business more than once. At times he's owed everybody and had no way, or so it seemed, of repaying anybody. His experiences can serve as encouragement and support to those who face major—or even minor—setbacks as they master their way to the top. For instance, Joe Sugarman went belly up when he was in his twenties, when his small ad agency was cheated out of an enormous sum of money by a client who turned out to be dishonest—who simply didn't pay for the agency's services. Joe is blunter than I; he refers to that client as "a crook."

Another time, Joe was left holding the bag when he developed a unique promotion for a TV program. It featured the

"Batman credit card," based on the program's main character, a fictitious "righter of wrongs." But he was denied a license to sell it, and he wound up with 250,000 cards. "I have them to this day," he states, showing that he still has a sense of humor about the experience.

There were other failed endeavors as well, including an electronics marketing business when he lost his competitive edge to businesses that were much larger, and as he endured costly battles against the Federal Trade Commission, waged in the press and in the courts.

Then Joe decided to start in a new direction, one that led him to his current business. He has prospered because he stuck to his belief that he would be successful, that success was the force that came from failure. He continued to treat customers fairly, to offer them the savings achieved from toll-free telemarketing or direct mail, and, through persistence, always paid back every cent he owed.

So I asked Joe Sugarman what advice he had for others who may have hit rock bottom in business, who were flat broke, who faced failure as he had. "Joe, I believe that one must realize that everything that happens in life is for the best. It may look at the time like the worst thing in the world, the darkest moment, but if you really believe that some good will come out of it, it will. I've found this to be true for me through years of experience and during many bleak moments. If you really believe that, you will find that it makes a big difference in life."

I asked Joe for advice he might give someone who may be undecided as to what career to follow or wondering how to get started in business. What about the very outset? His advice was basically not to worry about it. "It's okay, there's no crime," he states, "in not knowing what you may want to do. It's panicking about it that's the crime. When the time is right for getting into something you really want to do, it'll happen. It'll be very obvious. In the meantime just experience a lot of things. Go with the flow."

Go with the flow, I like that. It reminds me of that equally sound advice—don't swim against the tide. "It's from the experiences in life," Joe Sugarmen continued, "that you start programming your mind and discover what you like and what you really want to do. You meet people and you meet opportunities. Luck is where opportunity meets preparation."

Preparation? "Our brains are like energy generators," he explains. "We're one of the rare species that can think about something and then create the energy to make that thing happen. All we have to do is decide what we really want—think about it, visualize it, and just let it go. Eventually you get it. Some of the most incredible 'coincidences' have happened to me as a result of that process."

When those coincidences happen they certainly are experiences to be valued. I know that is true in my life and business career. Likewise, Joe Sugarman has had many rewarding experiences in his personal and business life. Helping people, he believes, has undoubtedly brought him tremendous satisfaction. Helping people achieve success has been the motivating factor in my books and lectures; I consider it a reason for being. To hear Joe Sugarman express a reason for his being is something I'll never forget: "I believe we're all put on earth for different reasons, and my reason for being on earth is to excite people, to get them to think differently from the ways they've thought before." To illustrate his philsophy, he related the following anecdote.

Plowing the Field

An editor and a friend drove into the Illinois countryside one afternoon. They both spotted a farmer on his tractor, plowing a field, going up and down the rows. The editor pulled over to the side of the road and stopped his car alongside a fence that bordered the field. He got out of the car, called out, and beckoned to the farmer, who stopped his tractor and came to the fence.

To the friend's surprise the editor began to berate the

farmer up one side and down the other. "Don't you know you're plowing your field so wrong? You must be a crazy guy the way you're plowing." The farmer, irritated, responded that he'd always plowed that way.

"You should be ashamed of yourself. Look at how dirty your tractor is." On and on went the editor. Of course, the farmer grew really upset and he started to yell and wave his arms. At that point the editor walked back to his car, got in, and drove off. His friend, still amazed, said, "I don't understand you. You were rude and you insulted that farmer. What's it all about?"

"Don't you see the good I've done?" the editor asked. "That farmer will go back to his home at the end of the day, and he'll tell his wife about the awful experience he had with a stranger and the injustice that took place. But what I did will get that man thinking—maybe something he hasn't done before.

"Maybe he'll start thinking that he might have been plowing his fields the wrong way, that perhaps he ought to change and get out of a rut. He'll talk to his wife and she'll sympathize with him. I hope I've stimulated that farmer to such an extent that I've changed his life for the better, that maybe he'll learn something from the experience and grow. I've got him off dead center."

Joe concluded his story by saying, "I feel that I was put on earth for that same reason—to communicate with people on a mass scale and in such a way that I arouse them, excite them, persuade them, and then provide them with a product that really helps them."

Unlike myself, who sold automobiles, on a one-to-one basis, Joe Sugarman does his selling one-to-a-million.

Advice from the World's Number One Ad Copy Man

Here is Joe's advice to young people who want to be in business for themselves and are determined to master their way to the top. It's equally good advice for those who want to advance in their organization and have their sights set on the top. Don't be afraid to use these ideas or adapt them to your own needs. He has always been copied, Joe states, and imitation is the sincerest form of flattery. That's why I say that if I can do it, so can you; and if Joe Sugarman can do it, so can you.

- Market a product or service that's unique. Look for that one-of-a-kind opportunity.
- Look for trends in what consumers are interested in and what they are buying.
- Advertise and excite in a manner that's as unique as your product or service.
- Be quick on your feet to outpace the competition.
- Appeal to the emotions of the customer. He or she is concerned about saving money, appearance, health, entertainment, and above all, value.
- Drop the product or service when your bottom line shows a loss in profits or competitive edge.
- Experience all the things that might happen along the way and get on with what you're doing. Go with the flow.

21
Try These Building Blocks

I'M SURE THAT at one time or another you've had a near accident, maybe an incident involving your car or a mishap at home or at work or while playing a sport. I know that I certainly have. Afterward, you probably breathed a sigh of relief and said to yourself, "Wow, that was a close shave!"

But there are close shaves and there are *close* shaves. It was no accident that an enterprising entrepreneur, a very successful businessman known in the United States and abroad, experienced a different kind of close shave. He was so impressed by it that he bought the company that made the product that supplied the shave. He told me, "I liked that shave so much that I flipped." He is Victor K. Kiam, chief executive officer of Remington Products, Inc., Bridgeport, Connecticut, manufacturer of Remington electric shavers for men and women.

For years Victor has been his own spokesperson on television, telling folks that "it shaves close as a blade or your money back." That promise is one of his guiding principles: Whatever your product, make sure it offers full value. But in addition to Remington, Victor owns a half dozen other major companies. His wealth and affluence today, as well as his home-and-abroad business influence, are a far cry from his first efforts, to earn money in a sales venture.

Fulfilling a Desire

Kiam was born in New Orleans, Louisiana, and was brought up by his grandparents. His parents were divorced when Victor was four, and had moved out of the state. His earliest business experience was at the age of nine, born of seeing a need and meeting it, of seizing a business opportunity and running with it.

"Back then," he told me, "I saw people getting off the streetcar named Desire, which actually ran a block from my house. We had no air conditioning back in those days, and the people were pretty hot and sweaty. Some of them would pass by my house, where I'd be playing in the yard." Looking at those hot and sweaty people, young Victor got the idea that maybe he could sell Coca-Cola to them. Meet a desire for something cold. He talked to his grandfather, who gave him five dollars. With it, Kiam set up a little stand outside of his house.

"I had a big tin filled with ice. I'd buy the Cokes for three cents and sell them for five cents." At the end of a month he saw that he'd lost money. His grandfather asked him how he could lose money. After all, there would have been two cents profit in every sale. Victor told him. "Some of the people are so poor they can't afford a Coke. I feel sorry for them and I give it to them."

His grandfather then gave him some advice about charity, which Kiam has remembered the rest of his life. "It's wonderful to be charitable," his grandfather told him. "It's the greatest thing you can be. But first you must make a profit. Then you can give the Cokes away."

Young Victor learned from his grandfather that, in order to do things that benefit others, whether in business or in private life, you must be financially able to do so. The seventeenth-century author Sir Thomas Browne stated it simply as "Charity begins at home." Some people today advise those who want to master their way to the top to "look out for number one." I like the way Browne stated it. I like the way Victor's grandfather put it even better.

The success stories of many men and women have humble beginnings. But just as all presidents aren't born in log cabins, all success stories don't begin in poverty. Certainly not Victor Kiam's.

As a boy, young Victor didn't suffer hardship or hunger. He wanted for little. Prior to the stock market crash of 1929, his grandparents were thought of as well off, probably upper middle class, but unfortunately his grandfather lost everything. At the height of the Depression, the grandfather rolled up his sleeves and found employment. He was a talented artist who, during nights, would sketch and paint. Later, at the age of seventy, he was hired as an artist and animator for Walt Disney Studios. "My grandparents were loving and kind," Victor recalls. "They really doted on me. I was probably treated better than a boy who had a mother and father living at home."

Still, there is a hardship that Kiam remembers: not having a mother and father during his early years. Victor Kiam left New Orleans at ten and spent two years in New York City living with his parents. Or sort of. The first year was with his father during the week and his mother on the weekends. The second year was the reverse. Finally, after those two years, he was on his own. From the age of twelve, Victor has stood on his own two feet.

Onward and Upward

Victor left for school at the beginning of his teen years, eventually going to Andover, a prep school in Massachusetts. Then, at seventeen he enlisted in the U.S. Navy. He was sent to officer training school, came out as an ensign, and then served on an aircraft carrier in the North Atlantic. The European war had ended, but the war in the Pacific was still going on.

When he got out of the navy at twenty, he began looking for a job. The best offers were in company mailrooms. Victor had nothing against mailrooms, but he was not interested. His military service qualified him for educational benefits under the G.I. Bill, so he decided to go to Europe, where he enrolled at the Sorbonne in Paris and, in time, received a certificate in languages. While in Paris he started his second business endeavor (the first being the Coca-Cola sales venture).

A newspaper man asked him if he'd like to take a gentleman and a lady on a tour of Paris. The lady turned out to be the gentleman's mother. They felt that the American Express tour, which at that time was $35 for the day, including car and chauffeur, was too expensive. The enterprising Kiam said he'd be very glad to give the couple a tour. He charged them $15.

Kiam's philosophy of "give a full measure of value" served him in good stead. The gentleman and his mother enjoyed the Paris tour very much. He turned out to be a professor at Smith College, the school for women at Northampton, Massachusetts. He recommended Victor to three young ladies from Smith who were traveling together. "I took them around in France and Italy for six weeks," he told me. Success in that venture gave him an idea. He created the European Touring Service, Inc. He had cards printed and went around to hotels in Paris looking for tour-guide business. His enterprise flourished, and at length he had a fleet of six cars, using other students at the Sorbonne as drivers.

At the end of the 1940s, Victor left the Sorbonne and enrolled in Harvard Business School. That's where, he told me, he got his push into the business world. Most of his fellow students had fathers who owned their own businesses or who were high-level corporate executives. "I wasn't in that position,"

Victor recalls, "yet I felt I was as good as the other students. They were all going to be 'successes' in business, and they had a head start. I simply was driven to be as successful as they were. I always wanted to win."

During a summer vacation, he went back to Europe and resumed his touring service at the height of the season. He recalls with pleasure an important French customer. "The Maeght Gallery and Museum had spawned most of the famous impressionistic painters. The gallery was located on the French Riviera, up in the mountains in back of Nice. I was the house chauffeur." At the Maeght Gallery he met and chauffeured such great artists as the Spanish surrealist painter Joan Miró, the Russian painter Marc Chagall, and many others.

"Where I got hurt," Victor told me, "was during the Korean War in 1951. Many Americans canceled their foreign travel plans because they were afraid there'd be a global conflict." He returned to Harvard, deciding he would not go back to Europe, and he sold his six-car fleet. "In those days the school viewed as a 'success' someone who left its hallowed halls, went to a major corporation, rose through its ranks, and became a power at that company. The idea of somebody doing something on his own was not as prevalent as it is today."

Working Smart

Victor Kiam went to work when he got out of business school. He took a job with the cosmetics division of a large company involved in international trade, a field he was interested in. But he worked stateside. Initially he was a trainee, then the company sent him as a salesman to a territory in Ohio. He had a hard time at first, but eventually he did all right because he worked seven days a week and lived out of a suitcase. Then he was "promoted" to cover five southern states. It was a big territory in which there had been a steady turnover of salespeople, so customers had gradually lost interest in the product line. He handled that obstacle by hard work—or, as you know I like to put it, by "working smart." He is frank to admit that one of the biggest problems he faced was when he'd question the way some things were done. The stock answer was "This is the way it's done; just do it!" And as usual, his immediate boss couldn't tell him why.

Victor Kiam didn't buy that. No way. "I would write in and say that something was wrong, why it was wrong, what I would do differently, and why I thought my idea was better." Challenging the this-is-the-way-it's-always-done mentality seemed to ring a bell, and he went up the corporate ladder very fast. Victor continued to point out better ways of doing things at the next company he joined and where he stayed for thirteen years. He started out as a regional manager, traveling throughout a territory that covered everything west of the Mississippi. Once again he lived out of a suitcase. "Then," he told me, "I was made marketing manager of one of the company's divisions and was brought to the New York headquarters. I continued up the ladder until I became executive vice president."

The Desire to Build

Kiam had mastered his way to the top by working smart, and most men would be satisfied to reach those heights—but not Victor Kiam. When, in the late 1960s, the parent company of his organization decided to put it up for sale, Kiam felt that the buyer was a financial player—a bean counter—and not a builder. "I'm essentially a builder," Kiam states flatly. By that he doesn't mean getting into the construction business. He means building a company, an organization, a business structure he could call solely his own. "I decided to go out on my own. A headhunter had offered me a job as president of a company, but then he told me, 'You know, Kiam, with your background you ought to be in business for yourself.' I took his advice."

So, at the end of the 1960s he got financial backing and took over an organization that had once been a well-known watch company, Wells Benrus. He ran it successfully for eight years, and turned it into a conglomerate. That's certainly light years away from selling Cokes for a nickel to thirsty customers getting off the streetcar named Desire.

Kiam added other business opportunities to his organization as well—for example, a precision-instrument component operation and a jewelry company. In fact, he and his wife had visited mainland China, being among the first Americans to do so after President Nixon paved the way. There they purchased and later sold a variety of beautiful mainland Chinese jewelry and artifacts.

Victor then sold his growing enterprise of Wells Benrus and bought Sperry-Remington, changing its name to Remington Products, Inc. The name is a natural, and it brings Victor Kiam's success story full circle.

He had heard that the company making Remington shavers was for sale, and had been keeping tabs on the company. His wife asked him what he was up to. "You've never shaved electrically," she said, "so how can you even consider it?" She bought him a Remington shaver as a gift and told him, "If you're looking at the company, at least you ought to try the product."

Victor told me, "I knew the only way to find out if the product gave full value was to use it. I tried it and I flipped. That's the 100 percent true story of why I bought the product and the company."

The Way to Treat People

I always like to know what spurs on successful people, what drives them despite obstacles and setbacks. Victor Kiam told me that people themselves were his spark. "I've always worked and associated with people whom I admired and respected, and through following that principle I gained, in turn, their respect—and that motivated me. I feel that people I deal with are in partnership with me." Kiam counsels that when you make mistakes, admit them and correct them. Never leave others holding the bag. Make your word your bond. "After fifty years of following those principles," he affirms, "I think I can go to anyone I've ever dealt with and be received with open arms." That might be the greatest success of all.

Kiam certainly followed a number of principles and techniques as he mastered his way to the top. He might not state them as formally as I see them, or in the same order, but as I review his story I am struck by his counsel. I recommend them to all who are blazing a career path. Because he is a builder, I see these as Kiam's building blocks:

1. Always want to win at what you do.
2. Associate with people you admire and respect.
3. Seek full value in products and services, and make sure you give full value in whatever you do.
4. Let charity to others go hand in hand with your success.
5. Treat whomever you deal with as a partner, not as an adversary.
6. Never leave people "holding the bag."
7. Keep an eye open for new business opportunities.
8. Look for better ways to do things, and show why.
9. Be competitive, and enjoy competition.
10. Be a builder!

If you were fortunate, you too might have had a grandfather who gave you counsel you've never forgotten. If so, add it to these principles and count your blessings.

22
Enjoy the Payoff

WE'VE COVERED A lot of ground in this book. You've learned how to know that you're number one. You've learned to dream big. You know the importance of setting realistic, achievable goals.

You've realized how much more time you have when you give yourself an extra month a year. You know the value of using that time wisely as you master the way to the top.

You know the importance of honesty.

You are aware of the necessity of associating with positive, upbeat people—people with ambition, people who are willing to roll up their sleeves and work smart.

I expect you have a belief in yourself that is stronger than ever before. And along with that belief, you should have faith in yourself. You should match that faith with faith in others.

You know that ambition can be a spark that drives you. You are going to be so self-disciplined that you'll be amazed how you control your life. You will no longer let others control you.

You will work smart every step along the way to the top.

And, you'll be tough on yourself whenever you have to be. But think of the rewards that lie ahead as you master your way to the top:

- Happiness in your chosen fields.
- Pride in successive achievements.
- Prestige, fame, recognition, awards.
- Financial stability.

Not all of us can be millionaires or billionaires, but I've cited a number of people who have achieved that measure of success.

Be Prepared for Change

No doubt you've set out on a long auto trip at some time or another. You got your maps at hand, your trip tickets. Then all of a sudden, you come to a detour sign—something that isn't on your map—and you're off on a course you didn't anticipate. Careers often have detours too, necessitating different plans, different steps to the top. Let me give you an example.

I had a long and prosperous career in selling motor vehicles. To me, salesmanship was a personally rewarding experience. I helped to put people in vehicles that were reliable, comfortable, safe, and affordable. But I had to face changes in my automobile selling career—for example, when it was no longer possible to sell cars in the Detroit area on Saturdays, one of the busiest days for selling. Remember, I wrote about that in Chapter 12. I also described the selling adjustments I had to make owing to the oil embargo in 1974. During those years there were many technological changes in motor vehicles, and as a salesperson, I needed to keep up with them. There is a lot more to selling cars than just asking for the order.

You must always be aware of and prepared for change. This

is especially true in selling a product, if selling is the career you're in, because each year, in every state, you can count on a flood of new regulations and laws. You must keep up with them. The day may come when salespeople, regardless of what they sell, may have to be certified the same way an auto technician is certified. In foreign countries where I have lectured, it's commonplace to see a sign in retail establishments that reads "Licensed to Sell."

You can count on these detours as you master your way to the top. Take them in stride. Remember, detours sometimes got you to see sights and scenery you might otherwise have missed. It's the same with changes in your steps to the top. Just stay focused on being number one.

Listen Up

Aren't you glad you are making the effort to master your way to the top? Aren't you glad you're number one? Successful living is living life to the fullest. It means living at the top. When you do, the other tops have a way of falling into place.

You can reach the top in your business, at your job, in your education, in your marriage, in raising your children, and in your play as well as in your work. Let me say it again: *If I can do it, so can you!*

Once there, you want to stay there. No one will topple you if you:

- Are absolutely honest in all your dealings.
- Keep informed on all new developments in your chosen field.
- Work smart.
- Keep your faith in yourself burning bright.
- Keep your promises.

- Manage your time wisely.
- Follow the Golden Rule to treat others as you would want them to treat you.

Know this, too: Even if you follow the advice above, there is a danger that you could topple yourself. Never become your own worst enemy. Aldous Huxley, the famed British author, once said: "There's only one corner of the universe you can be sure of improving, and that's your own self."

Let me share a poem written by my good friend Roger Dally. Roger is chairman of the board of Aloe International Distributors, which manufactures and distributes aloe vera health products, beauty products, and vitamins. The aloe vera plants are grown in Mexico. Roger has them shipped to the company's headquarters near Chicago, where they are compounded. A multilevel marketing operation, Aloe International has 10,000 distributors, operating in Mexico, Canada, Korea, Saudi Arabia, and Taiwan.

Born poor into a large family, Roger always had a strong belief that anything he would focus on strongly, he would be able to achieve. As a young man he earned money mowing lawns, delivering newspapers, and working in a factory that manufactured photo albums. Intuitively he knew he wanted to be in business for himself. He started his aloe business in his basement, then in his garage. People lined up in his driveway to buy his products, which he bottled and labeled himself. Later he mortgaged his home and borrowed from wherever he could in order to develop the facilities he needed. His company is now a $10 million business and is still growing.

His philosophy? Roger believes that too many young people miss the boat; they procrastinate going after what they want in life. I put a Girard spin on that, saying that too many people miss the target—the whole target, not just the bull's-eye. Roger cites the familiar phrase, "Ready, aim, fire!" He believes that taking too long to get ready is a mistake. Just *aim and fire* is his motto. Go for it!

A little guy when he was young, Roger mastered his way past bullies by being fast on his feet. Being fast on his feet also helped him become a champion tennis player. Being poor, the best he could afford was a $1 tennis racquet. He played another champ, a wealthy guy who had the best equipment and the finest tennis garb, and who drove to the court in a limousine. Roger aced him in short order, showing that wealth doesn't make you a champ.

Roger is wealthy, but he believes that you should not judge yourself by how much money you make, but by how much money you can help others to make. No wonder he has so many loyal distributors. Today, Roger is enjoying the payoff by starting to channel his time and resources into helping kids in the inner city—kids who need a guiding hand, who need someone to give them hope in life.

I believe in Roger Dally's philosophy of "Don't waste time, don't miss the boat." I believe in his advice to just aim and fire. The philosophy expressed in his poem played a big part in his success.

With his permission, I'm proud to share his poem with you.

Fly Like an Eagle

It's the fear of failing
that scares the best
and the fear of winning
that frightens the rest.

We make ourselves late,
We trip ourselves up.
Why be a winner
when getting by is enough?

I'd have to buy a big home,
drive a nice car.

Changes like these
are going too far.

Let someone else
earn all the money.
I'm content as I am.
I seem to have plenty.

But wait, just a minute
I've had some success.
And to be perfectly honest,
it felt good to be best.

If others can do it
so can I!
I'll stop making excuses.
I'll do it or die.

There's got to be room
for one more guy
to soar like an eagle
high in the sky.

So this I promise.
I'll get off my knees.
I'll start aiming high
where I know I should be.

I'll fly like an eagle
brave and free.
If you believe in your
    dreams
come fly with me.

Stop the World!

Some years ago there was a hit Broadway musical that is still often presented at dinner theaters. It was called *Stop the World, I Want to Get Off!*

My question is why? Instead of saying stop the world to get off, I say I want to get *on!*

Don't drop out of life or out of the business world when achievements can be yours. Reach out and grab the brass ring. *I know you can do it*. I'm rooting for you.

I wish you all the success in the world!

Index

About the Author

Joe Girard has always believed that smart work and persistence can work wonders, and he has proven this premise with his own life. Starting as a shoeshine boy, Joe Girard worked as a newsboy for the *Detroit Free Press* at the age of nine, and then as a dishwasher, delivery boy, stove assembler, and home building contractor before starting a new career as a salesman with a Chevrolet agency in Eastpointe, Michigan. Before leaving the agency he sold 13,001 cars in his fifteen-year career, including 1,425 cars in 1973, a record that put him in *The Guinness Book of Records* as "the world's greatest salesman" for twelve consecutive years. He still holds the all-time record for big ticket retail sales, an average of six sales a day.

One of America's most sought after speakers, Joe Girard appears before civic groups, religious organizations, and sales conventions of major corporations. His list of engagements includes such important companies as Brunswick, General Motors, Sea Ray Boats, Hewlett-Packard, Ford Motor Company, Sears, CBS Records, Kraft, Ameritech Publishing (Yellow Pages), Polaroid, Dun & Bradstreet, Kiwanis Clubs, National Home Builders Association, John Deere, Federal Reserve Bank of Chicago, National Home Furnishing Association, K Mart, Mary Kay Cosmetics, Chrysler Corporation, General Electric, 3-M, International Racquet & Sports Association, IBM, and several hundred advertising and sales clubs worldwide.

It is easy to understand why Joe Girard's first bestselling book, *How to Sell Anything to Anybody*, helped millions of salespeople all over the world, for it is here as well as in his following books, *How to Sell Yourself*, *How to Close Every Sale*, and *Mastering*

Your Way to the Top, that Mr. Girard reveals the secrets of his success: "People don't buy a product, they buy me, Joe Girard."

Mr. Girard's list of awards is exceptional, including the Number One Car Salesman title every year since 1966, as well as the Golden Plate Award from the American Academy of Achievement. He was also nominated for the Horatio Alger Award by Dr. Norman Vincent Peale (author of *The Power of Positive Thinking*) and Lowell Thomas, the *World's First Radio Broadcaster*. Joe Girard is always interested in hearing from his readers and may be reached by writing or calling:

> JOE GIRARD
> P.O. Box 358
> Eastpointe, MI 48021
> (810) 774-9020